THOSE AWKWARD
ONE DRIVE
STANDS

WHAT REALLY HAPPENS IN A RIDESHARE CAR?

ANDY VARGO

Illustrated by E.C. VARGO

Enjoy the Road!.
Andy V.

Your Awkward Life Gets Better

Text copyright © 2018 by Andy Vargo

All Rights Reserved

ISBN 9781097243709

Awkward Career Publications

awkwardcareer.com

Table of Contents

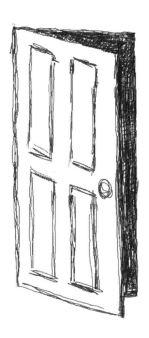

Preface

Everything had to start over. I had done this before, but somehow starting from scratch at eighteen years old seemed much easier than starting over at forty.

When you are forty there are some added obstacles, financial responsibilities, slower body, aging brain, which all hinder the ability to jump in with two feet and just make things happen overnight. But I ignore these and jump anyway. My life depends on it at this point. When the building is on fire, you jump out of the window knowing you can fix the broken bones later.

I jumped. In fact, I jumped far, telling my wife of nineteen years, that I was a gay man. Sharing this meant everything would change. Life would be starting over for me in every way. Knowing I will soon have no place to live and no ability to afford one beyond my responsibility to keep my wife and kids housed and fed, I turned to the quickest way I could find to make some fast money, being a rideshare driver.

As you can guess, it was the darkest time in my life. In the course of the last year, I had lost my job twice, started a divorce, and was now scared, broke, lonely, and in need of money quickly. So, I decided to do what all the cool kids do, become a rideshare driver.

I have a number I need to hit, and from all the questioning I have done, I should be able to hit that number driving on nights and weekends. My life is changing fast and I am grasping at anything to take control.

I did not, however, expect that this short term money grab, would take me down a path that would give me social fulfillment, financial freedom and even more, realize a life-long dream I have had to publish my own book.

As a rideshare driver, you get lots of questions and sometimes become a counselor to the general public. I at times feel there should be an extra button to bill for a mobile counseling session, "That will be $5.45 for the ride, plus $75.00 for listening." But that is just the entrepreneur in me working on more ways to make money.

Sure, I get asked a lot of questions, but the most frequent and most enthusiastic is the "Got any crazy stories?" question.

This question has become the premise of this book, the base of my impromptu stand-up act, and the center of conversation at parties in general.

Not everything I will share in this book is like an episode of *Rides Gone Wild*, but there is definitely a share of crazy in here. I have tried to make it as classy as possible, however, the general public is not always a classy bunch so when in doubt I have stayed truer to the event to give you a real feel of the nights out on the town.

There is another, less crazy side to driving. These are the genuine, really cool people that I have met throughout the Northwest, whether visiting or natives, I have met a lot of really great people traveling through our neighborhoods. These are the people that have left me wondering whatever happened to them. These are the people that did not call the morning after and these are the people that I feel left me with a One Drive Stand.

A Note About Names & Locations

The names of passengers in this book have been changed to protect the innocent. The locations visited are true, however, those have been mixed up as well, in order to protect the privacy of the passengers and where they may have been. The conversations, comments, and interactions with my passengers were not recorded. The conversations and quotes in this book are from my best recollection of the conversations had along the way. But I do have a very good memory!

Night One

It has been a long day. I have made my way back from Spokane and been in the car since noon. But I just received my clearance to drive, and want to test it out as soon as possible. Besides, it is Friday night, which from what I hear is one of the big money-making nights to be out driving.

So, for the first time ever, I push the icon at the top of the screen to 'Go Online' and drive around waiting for the signal to call for a ride. It does not take long, and I am on my way to the Edison City Alehouse to pick up Cody, my first rider ever.

Flinging his messenger bag over his shoulder, he holds the door open for someone entering, as he leaves the bar. Though I pick him up at a bar on a Friday night, Cody is not sloppy drunk, or even buzzed for that matter.

"Andy?"

"Yes, Cody right?"

"Yep." He lets out as he steps into the front seat.

Reaching forward to push the icon on my phone to start the trip, I share, "You are my first passenger"

"Just getting started for the night?"

"First passenger ever."

"Oh wow! What got you into being a driver?"

"I am actually just at the beginning of a divorce, so I am hoping this will help me pay the rent now."

"Well I am not going too far but it should be an easy and quick few bucks for ya."

"That is cool. How do you like that bar? I have not been in since they opened."

"It's a nice spot, I was actually there studying."

"Awe, what are you going to school for?"

"I am majoring in criminal justice, I would like to be an investigator."

"That's awesome, my son hopes to be a police officer someday and is working towards that goal now."

And before I know it, four minutes and three miles have passed under our conversation, bringing us to a couple of blocks from Cody's home. As we turn the last corner, my phone lights up with the signal for my next ride.

"Looks like you are off to a busy start!"

"Yes, so it appears."

"Thanks for the ride!"

"Thank you for requesting one!" and on Cody walks to his front door and off I go to my next call.

My next pick up is only about a mile from where I left Cody. However, the last turn I took to my pick up location seems to take me around the corner into sketchville. The dark house seems longing for a caring touch, cold and without the extra coat of paint so desperately needed.

I cannot see any signs of movement or life through the dark sheets covering the windows. Yet the driveway is packed with cars, though none of them appear to have been moved for quite some time.

There I sit waiting for my passenger, Jakob.

Soon two young men begin to wade their way through the dry overgrown jungle of the front yard towards my car. Their very presence begs for a challenge from society to push them to conform: pants seemingly falling to the earth as they walk, hair which can only be described as two-day bedhead. All pulled along with a careless slow stroll that comes with the privilege of having no particular place to be on time.

"Dad- you can't be a rideshare driver, that's sketchy! People sitting in your back seat that you do not know, cannot see, and do not have control of!" The words of my son are haunting me now as my second ride is far from the clean-cut, cheery conversation I just shared with Cody.

"Hi, Jakob right?"

"Yes." Before they can take their seats, my nose awakes to a very distinct, pungent odor: pot. "Do you see the address I loaded?"

"Yes, Lakewood right?"

"Yeah"

Pulling forward to get on our way, and knowing the area well, I see that we are going from sketchy to sketchier. The thought of what I could be hauling, besides passengers, creeps into the recesses of my mind. How easy would it be for an illegal substance or weapons to be a stowaway for the trip? "Well, I need the money." I tell myself.

Occupying only the back seat with an empty front passenger seat, no words are shared between them. Being a gentleman, I do not interrupt the silence myself until we arrive at their destination.

"Where would you like to be dropped off?"

7

"Right over there" The one I imagine to be Jakob, and the taller of the two, responds as he points to a break in the chain link fence where it appears a gate is meant to be.

"Alright, here you go. Thanks."

"Thank you." Jakob lets out, as he and his friend gain their footing on the ground outside the car, taking everything with them except the stinging smell of weed.

Rate Jakob appears on my screen as I end the trip. I can choose one through five stars. I pause and think about it. The pot smell was unpleasant, the neighborhoods were sketchy and I was a bit nervous. Then I take a closer look at my time with Jakob and his friend. Neither of them was rude. They did not make me wait, and in general, he held up his end of the transaction without incident. "No reason not to give him a five." I say to myself as I click the five-star rating.

"Now what?" I think to myself. I finished my first two drives and that was all there was to it. No email to follow up on. No voicemail to return. No homework. Just follow the line on my GPS, drop them off, and that is all I have to do. This is way too easy.

I do some math about what I have made so far. I am at $15 already with thirteen minutes of driving time in. At this rate, I am making over a dollar per minute. Of course, I know that I will not drive every minute and that I am not getting paid between riders. However, this is still a promising number.

It will be a few minutes before my next ride. Fifteen minutes with the windows down letting the fresh air blow through the car so that the next passenger does not think I just lit up.

Next, I head over for a pick up at the Tacoma Mall. Through the course of the night, I will give a store clerk a ride home from the mall at the end of their shift, a couple a ride to dinner, and a gentleman a hop from the downtown bars to the Half Pint, a bar on 6th Ave known for their fun atmosphere and great pizza.

I am not ready to make it a full late night, so around nine, I start driving towards home. I do leave myself online, however, figuring that if I get another call I can do one last ride.

Less than a mile from home, my phone lights up one more time. This pick up is only a few minutes away, so I might as well accept it, although after driving home from Spokane across the pass, I have already been in the car for nine hours by now. Looking forward to being home, I figure a few more bucks and a half hour later will be no big deal.

Parking in front of a completely dark house, I wait for Gale to come out.

Five minutes pass so I send a text.

"Just confirming I have arrived."

Nothing.

As I reach up to cancel the trip and call it a night, I see the front door open as light from inside spills out onto the sidewalk.

As Gale enters the car, I start the trip only to see for the first time that she needs to go to downtown Seattle. I did not anticipate people going quite that far with a rideshare ride. My mind was a mix of excitement to see what I would make on this fare in contrast to my desire to get home and rest.

Gale turns out to be an elevator passenger. You know the type, an elevator passenger is someone who speaks only as much as necessary: "Hello…Excuse me…Thank you…Goodbye." They are not rude necessarily, just not interesting, in fact very boring, and at times, downright awkward. It really is an interesting phenomenon that the same distance can be made to feel twice as long when in awkward silence. But alas eventually our elevator ride comes to an end as we reach the top floor and I let her out.

$46.29, good trip to end the night on. It was worth the awkward silence. Had it been another night, had I not already been on the road for over nine hours, had I not driven from Spokane to Tacoma, then all around the South Sound, up to Seattle and back, had I felt fresh and lively, I would keep the meter running and see what else I could get in. But for me, making $79 in a few hours was a good first night.

Mark the Groper

The road comes to a dead end hidden amongst the busy blocks of homes in the hilltop neighborhood of town. This is a quiet little community hidden behind the busy life of a growing city. I have never been to this block before and am surprised to see the little development of condos tucked away in their own little oasis behind the rest of the city neighborhoods.

As with every ride, I wonder what he will look like. All I know now is that his name is Mark, and he needs to be picked up right here.

Parked with my hazards on I watch for signs of life. It is a condo, so there are multiple people coming in and out. Often times I wonder if the others see me as a stalker just sitting in front of their home as I look at everyone with a gaze of 'Are you going to get in?'

Soon Mark approaches. I am sure it is him by the direct line he is making from his door to my car. And he is a great looking guy. When I say great, I mean great in all the sensible ways too. Not a shallow, beach body and fake tan way, but a good looking, nice guy that you can bring home to family, have a great conversation with and still be

11

enamored enough to want to have a hot make-out session with at the end of the day. What I am trying to say is, he has a really great smile and I think he is cute.

"Mark?"

"Yes, Andy?"

"Yes. How are you today?"

"Great, I am heading down to Rock the Dock to catch up with some friends I have not seen in a long time."

"Oh, that sounds like a lot of fun."

Rock the Dock is a bar tucked into the corner of a commercial building that has a pier-like feel on the water. It is a fun spot that is tucked away from the rest of town at the far end of the waterway from the marina and just below the buzz of downtown.

"Yeah, they have asked me to join a couple of times when it wouldn't work out, so tonight I was determined to make it happen even though it's a work night."

"I like this block you live on, I have not been back here before. It's a nice little hidden gem."

Mark goes on to tell me all about the condos, how they were repurposed from an old apartment complex, and how he found the place and fell in love with it right away. Then breaks in with, "You can stay in the right lane and go down 15th." He speaks in a helpful caring tone, not a demanding bossy way.

"Yeah, I grew up here so I am pretty familiar. Rock the Dock is a fun spot." I add like the geek I am, not knowing what else to say. I really feel chemistry and a connection with Mark even though we are not talking about anything of consequence. At least as much chemistry as you can feel through a conversation over your shoulder with a man in the back seat. But I can feel his warmth in the car and I can hear his smile. Not to mention the piercing look in his eyes coming through as he speaks.

Pulling up to Rock the Dock I turn to look back and say goodbye to Mark. He leans toward me. My heart races with excitement as I have no idea what is to come next.

Feeling the warmth of his hand take my shoulder under his control his lips open and he lets out, "Your tag is sticking out."

As he fixes my collar and releases his grip, he opens the door saying "Have a great night."

"You too! Thanks for getting a ride."

I pull away as my life settles back into the hopes and regrets which I live with every day. Hope that I will see him again someday. Regret that I did not speak up, that I did not ask what else he might be thinking. Was this just one more in a long string of missed connections, or maybe it was one more in a long line of misinterpreted actions.

This is only one of the 'one drive stands' that I will look back on with regret.

I will never know.

Blue

Lily walks towards the car. Her blue hair is the first thing to announce her presence. Next is her height, standing at a healthy six foot four.

"Thanks for getting a ride. There is a lever on the left side to let the seat back for more room."

"Thanks, and thanks for picking me up." Her deep voice contrasts her long hair and high heels, though it is not a surprise given her broad shoulders and straight lines.

"Where would you like to go?"

"Oh I'm sorry, I'm entering it right now. But you can head towards South Tacoma."

"Sure thing. How is your night going?"

"Good. I am tired though, I was just at the bar and ended up helping my friend bartend because they were short-handed and got slammed."

"Oh, good thing you were there and able to help. That was nice of you."

"Thanks. We used to work together so it was easy to jump in."

"That makes sense. I would be lost behind a bar."

"Thank you for your acceptance, not everyone is very understanding or open." She says a bit softer than before.

"I don't mind blue hair." I reply with a sly grin.

Lily returns a smile with a half laugh.

"Do you have a lot of people who are rude to you around here?"

"Well, this is one of the better places to live as a trans person for sure. But there are always people who just do not know what to say or how to act."

"I have always lived here, but it seems like the west coast would be ideal to be for more acceptance."

"The Seattle area has one of the top cultures for the trans, not just gay culture, but specifically the trans community."

"That makes sense, though I am still learning a lot myself." I choose not to share that I am gay. This is her ride, not mine.

"Well, the top four cities for trans culture are San Francisco, Orlando, Denver, and Seattle. Not necessarily in that order."

"I have been to Denver a couple of times for work, but not spent much time there otherwise. That one surprises me, but honestly, that is just my own stereotyping of Denver as a cowboy town."

"It's actually way more progressive than you would think. Oh, can we go through the drive-thru?" She points ahead to McDonald's.

"Sure thing."

"I was planning to get some food, but since I ended up working I never got a break until it was too late to get food downtown."

"No worries. I know the feeling."

"I have been to Denver a few times, it is a great city. You really should check it out sometime, other than work."

"Thanks, I will have to do that!"

A large Dr. Pepper, ten piece nugget, and large fry later, we are pulling around the corner from the drive-thru and onto her street.

"Right here with the chain link fence."

"Perfect. Thank you for getting a ride, and for all the info."

"Thank you, you're cool."

"Have a great rest of your night."

"Thanks, you too!"

The next thing I know, Lily unfolds her tall body out of the passenger seat and onto the curb, carrying her food and Dr. Pepper up to the dimly lit front porch an on with her life.

The Responsible Drunk

"Do you have something for my friend?" Keenan asks as he leans into the car, helping his friend into the back seat.

I do not know what he is talking about, "Is this a drug reference" I wonder to myself. Then I turn to see the full state of his friend. Now his question makes sense.

"Oh, you need a bag?" as I reach for the puke bag I keep tucked next to the driver's seat, so it is always within immediate reach.

"Thanks, you're the best! I am paying for a rideshare ride to get my friend home and then I'll have you continue on to drop me off." He explains. "Brian, what's your address?"

"Two…"

Then silence. Brian is almost out.

"Do you know what city I should head towards?"

"Dupont."

"Okay, well that gives you about fifteen minutes to get the street address out of him"

I pull away from Jazzbones, a club on Sixth Avenue that has live music weekly and draws a crowd on Thursday nights which never seems to have a hard time having fun.

"BRIAN! What's your address?"

"Two…"

Pause

"One…"

Silence

"Four…"

Silence

"Five…"

Deep breath.

"BRIAN!"

"Huh"

"What street?"

"G…"

Pause

"R…"

Silence

"A…"

Breath

"N…"

Pause

"T…"

"So it's 2145 Grant?"

"Mm… Hmm…" And then silence again.

Meanwhile, I get to know Kennan a bit.

He shares with me that he and Brian had been friends in high school.
At a stout twenty-three, Kennan had recently finished his run in the Air
Force and was out for a night on the town with his old friend. The ride
from Sixth Avenue to Dupont is a full twenty minutes and while
Keenan was not sloppy wasted, he does have a good talkative buzz
going.

"I do not know why but I am always taking care of everyone else.
Even when I am drunk I have to be the responsible one." Keenan shares
how much he really misses the friends he made in the service back in
Georgia. "The crowd was just different there than my friends here. It
seems hard to settle back in and find a crowd of like-minded folk,
though I am glad to be back home with family. And the weather is so
much better here."

He was staying with his folks and appreciates how well his Mom has
welcomed him home and allowed him a place to stay while he makes
his way back into civilian life and starts a new career.

"It is a tough choice right now. Do I go to school to pursue more
education, or do I just take a full-time job right away?"

Ungratefulness is not a trait that he would carry lightly, but he would
like to get out of the family home sooner than later.

"I should check in with Mom soon. I'm surprised she has not called."

As we wind up the hill towards Brian's place, I hear more about the comradery of the military and the friends back in Georgia that Keenan wishes were here. "There was never any drama, and you knew they had your back."

"It looks like this should be it on the right." The street numbers are hard to read at 1:45 am, and I am reluctant to shine my tactical flashlight at people's homes. "Is it this one right here?"

"I've never been to his place"

"Oh? Is that his car?"

"I do not know"

"Well this is the address he gave us"

"Brian! We are home buddy"

Silence

Keenan gets to the back passenger door. Tapping his silent friend on the shoulder he says again. "We're here." Now shaking his shoulder he tries again. "Brian-come on."

His arms wrap around his friend as he takes matters into his own hands and extrudes Brian from the back seat.

I observe from the front, questioning where the line from non-involved rideshare driver blurs with being a compassionate human being. A question I find myself constantly pondering.

As they start their three-legged race from the car towards the house it is quickly evident that Brian is dragging Keenan down. In a slow-motion sprawl, they end in a position of defeat on the front lawn just a few feet from the car.

Keenan does not take defeat as an option.

"Brian, fireman's carry. Brian, I am gonna do a fireman's carry."

And in one graceful motion, Keenan bends over, picks Brian up over his back, and immediately follows the same path of motion until they are both back on the ground with Brian's head landing on the side of the wheel.

"Just click end trip and go!" I hear non-involved rideshare driver say to his more compassionate human counterpart in my head.

"Does he live with anyone?" I ask.

The next sound heard by the empty street was a loud knock at the front door while Brian lay resting his passed out head against the tire.

Thud, thud, thud.

"WHO THE FUCK IS IT?"

"It's Keenan"

"KEENAN WHO?"

"I'm here with your son!"

"WHICH ONE?"

"Brian!"

The father opens the door, and I am just glad to see that in his silhouette there is not an outline of a shotgun.

"What the hell is wrong? Is he just drunk?" The father is a commanding figure who has either dealt with this before or simply has no patience for it whatsoever. "Get in here boy! You better not puke in my house!"

By the time he is finishing his sentence, Keenan had managed to get Brian to his feet and to the front door. The father did not touch his son.

Through the window, I can see the outline of Keenan gently laying his friend on the couch and covering him with a blanket, still holding the puke bag I had given him at the start or our trip.

The father still standing on the porch, surveying his property for intruders, appears as a farmer chasing coyotes away from the hen house.

I walk slowly up to the porch towards the father. The compassionate human is taking over the conversation in my head by this point. "Here you go sir, these are your son's glasses and hat. They fell off in the yard"

"Thanks." rolls softly off the father's lips.

I head back to the car to wait for the responsible drunk to make his way back so we can get him home.

"Oh, my mom did call" as he settles back into his seat. "Excuse me while I call her back. But just start heading out of the neighborhood and I'll give you directions to my place."

The next conversation I only pick up half of, but sometimes we only need to hear half of what we hear to get the point.

"Hi Mom"

"What's up?"

"Mom. I am drunk." This turns into the slightest laugh.

"Mom, I'm drunk. But it's okay, I'm in a rideshare."

"What Mom?"

"You're drunk too?"

"Where are you, Mom?"

"I don't know Mom! Where are you?"

"Text me the address Mom. Can you do that?"

"Mom, just text me the address."

"Can you text the address to me Mom?"

"Bye Mom"

"Looks like we need to go pick up my mom too?"

By now we have found our way out of the neighborhood of the angry father and poor Brian. Keenan navigates me towards Lakewood which is about ten minutes back in the direction we already came from.

Soon a text comes in which we load into the GPS. I know the area well and this is a residential street. She must be at a friend's.

"There, that's my mom's car. That is my mom through the window. I will be right back."

After a brief stop, out comes the responsible drunk and his wobbling mother. She is not a crazy sloppy drunk, however, I do watch as she takes a couple of hard steps and gives the surprised look of one who has had a bit too much when their foot lands solidly on the ground about six inches sooner than they expect it to touch down.

Situated back in the car now, I start to take directions from Keenan on where to go. "Go left up at the stop sign."

"Right here---"

"No Mom! Let me give directions. Go left up there at the stop sign"

"I know that son. Right here, I was going to tell you, is where I pulled out in front of a cop a couple of weekends ago, coming back from Rita's house."

"Were you drinking then Mom?"

"Yes. And that is why I am in a rideshare now. It's too risky!"

"Did he pull you over?"

"Yes, I cut him off. He pulled me over and asked if I had been drinking. I said 'No Sir.' You never admit fault." To this, a slight snigger escaped her lips. "He says, 'Can you think of a reason why you pulled out in front of me like that?' and I told him no sir!"

"Mom!"

"But he didn't give me no ticket! But I am not gonna risk it again. No sir!"

"That sounds like a good idea." I confirm.

A right turn, a left turn, another right turn into a long driveway and finally Keenan, the responsible drunk, is home with his mom, and I am on my way to the next call.

Underwater Adventures

When I tell people that I am a rideshare driver, the first and often only thing they think I do is drive drunk people home from bars. That surprisingly is far from the truth.

While the partiers always need rides and they can be a big part of my business, many people simply need a ride to or from work, to run errands or even to the hospital. As a driver for hire, I have come to meet people from every walk of life that I may not otherwise have the chance to meet and even if we did, I would not have the alone time to learn about the amazing lives they lead. You will find many of their stories throughout these pages and Steven's story is a great place to start.

Pick up Steven rings through on my phone. The address looks eerily familiar. It only takes a minute for me to realize that he is right down the block from my sister's house.

Pulling into the familiar neighborhood, I glance at her place as I pass by, figuring I'll give an obnoxious honk and wave if the chance presents itself. Seeing no sign of life in the front of her home, I roll past and pull into the drive at the address for Steven.

"Hey there, how are you?"

"Great, just heading out to get Sushi. I am visiting and borrowing a friend's car for the day while I am here. But I had a beer a couple of hours ago and his car has an ignition interlock system so it won't start."

"Oh man, I did not realize how sensitive those machines are, but I guess that is a good thing."

"Yes, I found out they have a very low tolerance level."

"So you are just visiting for a bit?"

"Yes actually, I am a diver and needed to come here to work in the tunnel."

In Seattle, they are working on a project to reroute the major highway that runs along the main waterfront area. Currently, this has been a viaduct that is a two-level highway which blocks much of the city view of the waterfront and is in need of repair to maintain the ever-increasing demand for traffic. The solution was to dig a tunnel and divert the traffic underground.

"So are they underwater where they are drilling? I did not think that was the case."

"No, actually it is dry. However, they have to pressurize the air ahead of the boring machine in order to not have it collapse. The minors cannot work in that environment because they are not trained to work in a pressurized environment. So they send in commercial divers."

"Wow! That is really cool. So what will you be doing?"

"Well, anything mechanical or construction related that needs to be done. Most people think of commercial divers as doing just underwater welding."

"Yes, that is what I have heard of and usually would think of, thanks to *Deadliest Catch,* mostly."

"That is what most people think. But we actually are trained to do everything that may need to be done in construction or mechanics. Anytime a project needs to be completed in a pressurized situation or underwater, we are called in. I've even used a chainsaw underwater before."

"Oh, that is awesome. So how does that work? Obviously, you can't fire up a gas engine under water."

"I use mostly hydraulic tools. We have to counteract the air pressure that we are fighting underwater. So using pneumatic tools would not work, the pressure is basically counteracted by the pressure against the machine underwater. By the time the air would reach the machine, it would not move the engine. With hydraulics, it works. Picture a chainsaw with two tubes attached to the end, one forcing pressure in while the other lets the pressure out the back end causing the chain to move along that flow."

Now it's time for a scientific disclaimer: I am sharing the memory of how this was explained to me. I may have jumbled the science and mechanics a bit in my recollection, but you get the idea.

"I love my job and never have a day where I feel like I go to work. I get to travel all over the world. Two weeks ago I was in London and once I am done here I will be going to Florida"

And with that, we pull up to Mandolin Sushi & Steak House, one of the great hidden spots in Tacoma for Asian Cuisine.

"Well, I hope you enjoy your meal and have a great trip! Safe travels."

"Thanks for the ride. Drive safe."

As Steven walks towards his sushi and steak dinner, I am left contemplating all the new information I just learned. I feel like I just finished watching a documentary or an episode of *How It's Made*.

Fools

It's refreshing to see Josh standing on the curb in front of his house. I know at least that I will not have to wait and hope I am in the right place.

"Hey there! Josh right?"

"Yes, thanks for picking me up."

"No worries. Just heading down to The Mix?"

"Yes, I was down there earlier but decided I wanted to stay and drink so I brought my car home before I started."

"Smart plan."

"Yeah, it is just better to plan ahead."

"I agree. I have not been into The Mix yet. I just came out a few months ago. It looks like a fun place."

The Mix is one of the two gay bars in Tacoma. Both of which are a block apart. The Mix is very laid back, more like a neighborhood bar with a gay twist to it.

"You just came out! That is really awesome. Congratulations!"

"Thanks. It was not easy, but it has been the best thing I have ever done for myself. The hardest, but the best."

"That is great. Well, you should come in and check it out sooner or later. It is totally a low key place."

"I will for sure. I have been doing a lot of new things since I came out. Started doing stand-up even."

"That is really cool. Have you ever done improv?"

"I have not. I bet that is fun though too."

"I run an improv group here in Tacoma and we will be looking for new members soon."

"Really? I am going to have to think about that."

I do not know why the idea of improv is scarier than stand-up to me. Maybe it is the need to think on your feet as opposed to having a planned set.

"We are called Fools Play Improv. We perform every month at Tacoma Little Theater."

"Nice. I will look you guys up and get to one of your performances for sure at the very least."

"That would be great. We have one every month at Tacoma Little Theater. And seriously think about coming down and trying out."

"I will think about that one. I like the idea of the challenge."

"We teach you everything you need to know, and we practice all the time."

"Really, how do you practice improv? Seems like that defeats the purpose of it being improv."

"True, improv is all about being in the moment and not rehearsing a planned performance. But you have to practice learning how to be in the moment."

"That makes sense."

"We practice things like, how to work together as a team with our group, and different styles of humor and entertainment."

"I guess those would all be important."

"Yeah, it is all about being comfortable together and on stage so that when we are in front of the audience, ideas flow naturally in the moment."

"I guess there really is a lot behind the scenes to any performance, more than you might know or appreciate up front."

"True. Well, thanks for getting me back down here."

"You are welcome. Thank you for getting a ride."

"Hope to see you at one of our events soon."

"For sure!"

It is three more months before I make it to Fools Play, but I will be back again soon. The team works together well, plays off the room, and takes you on a journey as they improvise through their night of entertainment.

Old School

By this time, I am not surprised to have the smell of weed be the first greeting I receive when the door is opened for a passenger to get in. However, I still can be surprised sometimes at who carries the smell with them.

They have to be in their late fifties, early sixties. I pick them up from what looks like quite a party at a rented hall on the top of the hill in downtown.

Downtown Tacoma is essentially built on one steep hillside with the main drag being Pacific Avenue, which runs along the bottom of the hill before you cross the water to the Port of Tacoma.

Everything seems to be funny for these two. Even the simplest turns, and especially the dips, in the road as we soar downhill, hitting all green lights along the way.

As we come to each intersection, the steep downhill grade levels out through each crossing. The force of the car flying down the hill, then leveling, then going down again, can give you the sensation of being on a roller coaster. Especially when you hit the timing right and are able to have a full run of green lights the whole way.

Laughing the entire way, Shannon just seems to be having a blast. They only need to get from the top of the hill to the bottom and around the corner to get to the Matador for happy hour and more after-party libations.

Kevin catches a glimpse of my jacket. It's a faux leather jacket with some stitching in the design that works its way around the collar and down the sleeves.

"Nice jacket!"

"Thanks, I found it on sale last year."

"Dude, It's really cool. I love it. Those stitches though, are sweet!"

"Thanks."

"I'd buy it from you."

"That is very cool of you, but I just don't see myself parting with it."

"I wanna feel it." Shannon giggles as she runs her fingers up the stitching along the back of my coat. "Look, I am fingering the rideshare driver."

"I can't say I didn't enjoy it." I banter back as I pull up to a red light.

"But how much would you give it up for?" Kevin pursues. "Fifty bucks?"

"I really can't imagine not having it. It is one of my favorites."

"Seventy-five?"

I think for a moment. This honestly is more than I paid for this jacket a couple of years ago, but still, trying to find another to replace it would probably cost a lot more, if I even found one that fit as nicely.

"I fingered the rideshare driver!" Shannon giggles through her memory. "I think you still are fingering me." The touch of her finger runs up the edge of my arm, made soft by the weight of the faux leather between us.

"So you gonna sell it?" Kevin tries again to take my jacket off my hands.

"Nah, sorry man, I just can't let it go. Looks like we are here."

"Alright. Can't blame a guy for trying."

"Not at all. Have an awesome night!"

"You too." Kevin gives me a ten dollar bill and away they go to the rest of their night and on to the rest of their lives.

But not before Shannon could shout out her last goodbye for all of Pacific Avenue to hear.

"Bye Mr. Rideshare driver. Thanks for letting me finger you!"

Off-Leash

"Your passenger ride has been requested through a third party service. Your passenger may be hard of hearing, have limited eyesight, may use a cane or walker, have a service animal, and may need special assistance entering or leaving the vehicle. If you cannot accommodate any of these needs, please press nine and we will cancel the ride."

This is not a very uncommon call to get when a ride is ordered through a third party. I consider this job to be a community service at times as much as anything else. I think it is great that there are options for seniors and others who have special needs to find a way around the city, to appointments and errands, even if they do not have a smartphone. Thanks to third-party services like this that will schedule the ride for them, they can get around.

The first time I received one of these calls, I was very curious to see exactly what combination of these potential needs I might encounter. Now I understand it to be more of a catch-all and typically only one, if any, of the potential needs really do come up.

"Ride for Sandy?"

"Yes, I am Andy, how are you today?"

Sandy starts to make her way out from under the cover at her condo, rolling one of those fancy walkers in front of her and a little Yorkie behind her.

"Come on Lady." The little dog seems to do her own thing and just sorta ends up going the right direction as the rope leash guides her along. "I gotta use the ramp."

Sandy is down two short flights of stairs. Up until this point, I was trying to do the math on how this situation was going to play out. The ramp was hidden from my sight behind a cement retaining wall shrouded with an evergreen hedge.

"Do you need a hand with anything?" When it comes to offering assistance, there is a respect and dignity owed to those who may need it in not assuming they cannot do anything, while still offering to help.

"No, I have it alright."

"Okay, should I pull my car over to the side?" Now that I can see the ramp, I notice she will be coming out around the corner and up the hill to where I am parked.

"Oh, that would be great."

She is quick up the ramp, her frail body seems to scuttle along just fine, while Lady seems to mimic her shuffle. By the time I have backed around the corner, Sandy is waiting for me where the ramp meets the road.

"Would you prefer to sit in the front or the back?"

"The back. You can fold this up by just pulling up on this bar right here."

Folding walkers, pulling apart wheelchairs and getting creative with crutches and canes has become a skill I did not expect to acquire with this job.

"We are going to Wag, on Proctor Street."

"Okay. Sounds great. That is a pet store right?"

I have driven past, but never had a reason to stop in. The family dog was really my daughter's pet more than anything. So while I do get to dog sit from time to time, I do not have to hit the stores for his everyday needs.

"Yes, I need to get her a new leash. Hers broke and I just have this flimsy one that she can get away from which does no good when the kids walk her. If she gets away, she will run."

"Oh I get that, that's how our dog is. I finally figured out when he takes off to just open the car door and start the car and he will jump in because he thinks we are going somewhere."

"What kind of dog do you have?"

"Well it is actually my daughter's dog, but he is a Pekingese and Toy Fox Terrier"

"What an interesting mix."

"Yes, he is twelve years old and still looks like a puppy."

"So you inherited your daughter's dog?"

"No, it is just that he is pretty much her pet." Explaining that we are divorced, the dog doesn't live with me, and that it really is my daughter's dog is just a lot to cover in a five-minute ride.

"We inherited pets from our kids. I have six kids and each time they would move out, they never took their pets. But I drew the line at rabbits."

"Yeah, rabbits would be a bit much to take care of."

"We seemed to have one for everything. We had a dog lover, a cat lover, a dog and cat lover, an anything will do, a big dog lover and then, of course, my son who got into rabbits."

"My daughter is a dog lover and then I have a son that would be in the anything will do category. He always wants to have reptiles and snakes."

"My daughter always seemed to bring a different pet home every week. She would beg to keep it since it just 'followed me home' and we would go through the dance every time. I would usually cave, but not my husband"

You can hear the love of animals in Sandy's words. "One time she brought home two big dogs, and my husband said it was him or the dogs. I had to think about it for two days."

"Oh no!" My nervous laugh gives away the fact that I am not really sure if she is joking about having to think about it for two days.

"We found a neighbor to take one and drove her around for a while figuring she would not be able to find her way back home. But sure enough a week later she got out and made it to our house. And she was in heat!"

"Uh oh."

"Right! Well, I put her in the basement and locked the door and told the kids, under *no* circumstances are you to let her out or to let Chip get down there. He was just…well he was just horny."

I have to laugh, and I can't even keep it to myself, to hear someone of such advanced youth use the word horny so casually.

"Well we got her back to the neighbors and sure enough sometime later the neighbor called and said they were delivering Chip's puppies. I do not know how they got together, but I went over and helped. Those poor puppies got all of Chip's worst qualities and none of the mom's good qualities. But still they were puppies, and of course, my husband would not let me keep any of them."

"Awe well, it sounds like you had a pretty full house still. But pets really can be great."

"Yes. I swore I was not going to get another one. They just break your heart when they die."

"You are right, people do not realize how connected you get to a pet. You can spend almost every hour of the day with them sometimes."

"I knew our Spaniel would die as soon as my husband did, they were so close. Sure enough, my husband passed and within a month she was gone too."

"I am so sorry."

"Thanks, it was really hard, even though I saw it coming. That is why I never thought I would have another dog."

"Is her name Lady?"

"No, actually it is Phoebe Marie."

"Awe, that is a pretty name. Looks like the store should be right here, have you been here before?"

"Yes, it is just past Knapps Restaurant."

Not seeing a sign, I go past where the store should be. The storefronts are dark and nothing stands out as a pet store. Making a u-turn we slowly explore the businesses as I stop in front of the address we had in the GPS for Wag.

"It should be right here."

"Oh no! Did they close?"

"Let me look it up on my phone to see if they list a different address."

"Oh, could you? That would be great. I really need to get her a leash." I can feel her stress growing as she thinks through what to do.

"Yes, it says that they should be right here where the *coming soon* sign is. There is another pet store over on 26th and Pearl I could take you to."

"That is so far, can you see if there is anything closer?"

Typing in pet stores near me, the list, of course, brings Wag up as the best result plus a couple of other options that were each about a mile or two away.

"Perhaps I should call them and see if they moved locations?"

"That would be great if you could!"

"Thank you for calling Wag."

"Hi, I was just wondering if you moved?"

"Yes, we did. We are just across the street. Well across from the Blue Mouse, so just down a block and across the street."

"Thank you, we will see you in a minute."

"Great! Thank you."

"Oh thank God!" The sigh of relief can be felt in the entire car as the fear and stress of Sandy's plans not coming together fade away.

One more u-turn and one block later, and Sandy is having me gently load Phoebe Marie into her walker as she shuffles into Wag to find the perfect leash.

What Next?

"Do you know why I pulled you over?"

"I believe I was going a little over the speed limit."

"Yes, you were going 42 miles per hour in a 25 mile per hour zone."

"Oh wow, I thought it was 35 right here."

"No. It's 25 for another half mile."

"Oh, I thought that was just through the Edison District."

South Tacoma Way is a four-lane road that stretches from downtown Tacoma all the way to Lakewood. Like Route 66, in its prime, it was the main route for traffic traveling north and south, before the introduction of the interstate. It boasts such historic landmarks as the World Famous Bob's Java Jive, a dive bar in a building shaped like a teapot, and the B&I, a local market that was once home to Ivan the gorilla.

South Tacoma Way is also home to the Edison District which has been awakening as one of the newest hot spots for nightlife with the recently renovated Airport Tavern and newly opened Church Cantina across from age-old favorites like Dawson's Bar & Grill and Stonegate Pizza & Rum Bar. All in all, it is a great mix of history and modern life.

"Where are you off to in such a hurry?"

"I am a rideshare driver and I just got a call for my next ride."

"I see."

"Ya, I saw he was just up the hill so I accepted the ride and sped up a bit."

"I wondered because I clocked you at 37 and then all the sudden you jumped up in speed."

"That's probably right when I took the ride."

"Makes sense now. I was mainly making sure you are not drinking and driving."

"No, not at all."

"Well sit tight and I will be right back."

Through my rearview mirror, I see the officer walking back as his silhouette is framed by a backdrop of blue lights.

Be there soon, I had a short delay. I text to Steve, my next ride.

"Here you go. Be careful to slow down through here."

Seeing only my license and registration now in my hand, I am relieved. No ticket.

"Thank you so much, officer! I will for sure."

"You're welcome. Drive safe."

"Thank you, and thank you for your service. Stay safe out there."

It is just a short ride up the hill before I am in front of Steve's apartment.

"Sorry for the delay."

"No worries, I am just glad that I could get a ride. I do not have a car for the next couple of weeks before I move."

"That can be tricky. Where are you moving to?"

"Well, to start I am going to head home to Georgia and then decide what to do. I am transitioning out of the service and really do not know what I want to do next."

"Hey, thank you for your service. That is a big change for you. I know lots of guys who have worked through that."

"I just finished being deployed too, and the really hard thing is that I felt like I was in the middle of everything going on the whole time I was in the service." Steve's words seem to drift off with his thoughts.

"I can only imagine."

"They even filmed a movie I was in part of. Have you seen Restrepo?"

"I have not watched it yet, but it is on my list to watch. A friend told me about it. That was in Afghanistan right?"

"Yeah, they were right there filming in the middle of everything going on."

"That is really awesome."

"So now it feels like the world has forgotten me. I was in the center of the conflict, right in the middle of what was being watched everywhere, and now anything else I do just seems to be less important."

"I can understand that. It is not easy when you do not know where to go next."

"Exactly. So do you have another job, besides being a rideshare driver?"

"Yes actually, this is just my side gig to fund my dream of being a writer and motivational speaker."

"That is awesome. What got you into that?"

"Well interestingly enough, I never knew what I wanted to do when I grew up. But I always knew I wanted to help people. And I love telling stories to inspire people either in writing or in person. So when I had changes at work that left me between jobs, I decided it was now or never."

"See that is so cool how you are just following your passion and making it happen."

"It has been the most rewarding thing I have ever done. Of course, it has not been easy."

"So what would you say to someone like me that is trying to figure it out?"

"Well, I would say that the answer is already in you somewhere, it may not be obvious, but you know what wakes up your soul. Finding it may just take some exploring and reflection."

"I suppose that makes sense."

"It took me a long time to figure it out, but once I did, it has made all the difference. I cannot say that I have not had any more challenges, but when you know you are on the right path, the stress is completely different."

"So how did you figure it out?"

"Well, I read a lot, and there are several great books that helped me find the answers. As well as conversations with friends and mentors."

"That is what I should start doing."

"I could recommend some great places to start if you like. Here's my card. If you email me I can send you a list of good books and some questions to think about."

"That would be great. Speaker, coach, comedian, eh?"

"Yes, that's me."

"What do you coach?"

"The coaching goes hand in hand with the speaking. My focus is on helping people through life changes as I have experienced so many myself."

"I definitely am there right now."

"Well if you wanna reach out, I am glad to catch up and share resources with you anytime. Just happy to help."

"Thanks, I will send you a note once I get settled. Right now I am getting all my stuff moved and trying to hang out with all my buds as much as I can before I leave."

The comradery of the military really is something I admire. My friends in the service, as well as the guys I meet driving, always refer to their brothers in service with such respect and closeness that I can only imagine is essential in a place where your lives are in each other's hands.

"Is that what tonight is?"

"Yep, I think there will be five or six of us there just hanging out. I was in for the night, but I only have a few more chances to be with these guys."

And with that, we are in front of The Forum. Whenever I have military guys going out, this is one of the top places they go. It is a fun lively bar in the heart of the nightlife on Pacific Avenue in downtown and always seems to have a packed house.

"Well thank you so much for getting a ride, and for your service!"

"Thank you, I will send you a note when I get moved."

"Awesome. Best of luck Steve."

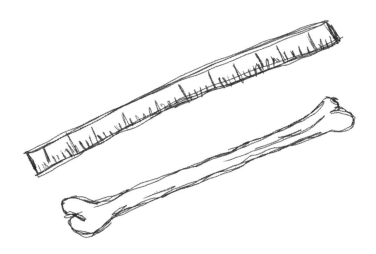

The Well-Endowed Skeleton

2:10 am the Saturday night before Halloween. Well, to be more accurate, early Sunday morning.

Bars are closed, parties are dying down, and I have about an 80% chance that anyone looking for a ride at this time has been the hardest partiers in the bar. The other 20% are the servers and bartenders that are wrapping up their night and are sober, and ready to get home.

I get a call to The West End, a local bar on an old strip of town that is not far from home. I know exactly where I am going. I have had one request from this location about two months prior and that ended in a rider no show at about 2:30 in the morning. I cannot help but wonder if this could be a repeat, but The West End is one of my favorite local neighborhood bars. It is the kind of place where you can walk in and feel like everybody actually really does know your name.

Pulling up to the bar I see a group waiting outside. At least I know I will have a passenger. This is prime time for fares so I am glad that it was not wasted on a no-show. The group piles in, two guys and two gals.

"Do you have a bag?"

"Of course! Here you go."

Not all of their costumes stand out, but one of the guys is dressed in one of those suites that are all black with the white bones of a skeleton painted on the front. He sits in the front seat.

"Are you Derek?"

"Yep, at least I hope so. You Andy?"

"Yes, thanks for getting a ride."

His girlfriend, dressed as a ho, sits in the back. At least I think that is what she was going for. There seems to be a movement in so many to wear as few clothes as possible and call it a Halloween costume. I am not sure if this is a costume, or just regular Saturday night apparel, now that I think more on it.

I say she sits in the back, but in reality, it is more of a crawl and lean. Crawl across the seat and lean on whoever or whatever is closest. Her other two friends help get her in and keep her close to the window.

She looks terrible. Can't keep her head up and is giving signs that she could vomit any second.

"Don't suffocate her!" Says Less Drunk Girl in the back, to Backseat Guy.

"I am holding the bag over her mouth so she doesn't puke in rideshare guy's car."

"You don't have to put it over her head."

"Well…"

"Can we stop at 7-11?" Asks Skeleton in the front seat.

A nervous "Sure" slips out of my lips before I consider the full extent of the situation in my backseat.

A few blocks away, the doors fly open in front of the convenience store and the two guys start to head into the store. The gals decide to get out for some air too. "Thank God." I think to myself.

As the usual late-night munchies are acquired in the store, the girls are wandering back and forth in the empty space next to the car. It is more of a lean and react than a stroll. Drunk Ho is putting all of her weight on Less Drunk Girl, and that causes a few quick steps in one direction while Less Drunk Girl struggles to support herself and the dead weight of her friend.

A moment later I hear a thud and an exclamation. Looking back over my shoulder I see both of them rolling off the back of the car two spaces over.

Less Drunk Girl pulls herself from Drunk Ho, though they stay connected at the fingertips. There are few sights more funny and sad at the same time than that of a drunk person trying to support an even more-drunk person.

In a rocking motion, as if you would do when trying to get your car out of a sand dune or snow drift, Less Drunk Girl tries to negotiate her weight in support of getting Drunk Ho off the ground.

I look back to the store to see if the guys are about done. They are at the register. In the full view of the glass door, I now see part of Skeleton's costume I had not noticed in the haste to get them home without Drunk Ho puking in the back. There, halfway up his costume extends about a foot long penis bone, for extra effect.

I laugh a little inside.

Noticing activity to my right again, I see the girls are successful in getting off the ground. Less Drunk Girl tries to get Drunk Ho into the back seat but as she lifts her leg to step in, the weight of her body tilts back against Less Drunk Girl. Less Drunk Girl, gives way to the weight and now Drunk Ho is laying on her back, legs facing the car as she rolls on the ground.

It is now that I notice how authentic her costume is, right down to the panties, or lack thereof. Yes, there they are, right in front of me, two bare ass cheeks wrapped in fishnet stockings like a holiday pork roast.

I can only hope that little bit of skirt wraps over those before they are placed back on my seat. Wishful thinking, I am sure.

Before long, Skeleton, Backseat Guy, Less Drunk Girl, and Drunk Ho are all back in their original seats and we are on the way. I am relieved to see that their house is only about a mile away.

"Can we run through Memo's?" asks the well-endowed skeleton.

I usually go wherever the rider wants to go and do not give them any issues or complaints about stops. But this is too risky. Memo's is an all night drive through with great Mexican food and it is just down the road, but the risk of an extra stop during one of their busiest times is just too big.

"Dude we cannot make any more stops!" comes from Backseat Guy with excitement.

"Oh alright, whatever."

I feel relieved. "I just noticed the rest of your costume while you were in the store. Funny!"

"Yeah, I feel bad because technically it is false advertising." Derek replies, as he reaches up and squeezes an air pump in his sleeve which activates the penis bone to surge up and down. I give a nervous little laugh and look back to the road.

Two long minutes later we pull up to their house.

Backseat Guy and Less Drunk Girl help extract Drunk Ho from the back seat. Fortunately, they take everything with them and leave nothing behind, except the lingering thought of a holiday pork roast ass being pressed against the seat.

It's time for me to sign off for the night and head home. I cannot risk the next one actually being a puker!

Change

This looks like the right place. The mailboxes are across the street and the house number is not visible from here, but I believe the coral colored house to the right is the one I need to be at. Stopping at the edge of the driveway I wait for signs of life.

Before long, the screen door opens as who I guess must be Jodene steps out to the front porch. She just looks at me. Why isn't she coming out to the car? Maybe this is not the right house after all.

It takes just long enough to feel awkward before she gives me a wave. Then I see that just beside her is a rolling suitcase. This must be an airport run. Now it makes sense, she is waiting for me to pull up the drive to pick her up.

"Hi, Jodene right?"

"Yes, thanks for coming."

"Of course, you are keeping me working!" closing the trunk, I settle into the driver seat. "Heading to the airport?"

"Yes, it's time to head home."

"Oh were you just visiting?"

"Yes, this is my mom's house."

Given that Jodene seems to be of advanced years herself, this takes me a bit by surprise. I would have expected her to be the mom visiting her kid. Just goes to show you cannot walk into certain situations with expectations.

"That is awesome, did you have a good visit?"

"We had a great time. She still lives in the house I grew up in."

"That is pretty neat. So how does that feel to come back and visit?"

"Well, I have been gone for several years. I moved to California thirty years ago and never moved back."

"Definitely long enough to feel like that is home now."

"Yes it does, but I will always have such fond memories of growing up here. I have actually planted a couple of evergreens in our backyard just to get the smell of home. You just cannot know how much a smell can bring you back to a memory or a feeling."

"That really is true."

"When I step out into the backyard, especially in the fall, the smell just awakens me, and I would never give up that connection."

"Are you able to come back and visit often?"

"More now that I am retired. It used to be once or twice a year, now I get to come up and visit with Mom almost every other month."

"You really have to take advantage of every chance to be with family that you can."

"You are absolutely right. Of course, this place has changed so much from when I grew up. I went to school there, and it was nothing like that back then." Jodene points to the University Place Primary School as we drive past. It has the look of a brand new school, but this is surely due to recent new upgrades. "Back when I was a kid this was all trees and hills as far as you could see. The houses were tucked under the canopy of the forest and looking from the top of the hill, you would never know they were there."

"It really has built up so much, even in just the last few years."

"Now, everywhere you look, all you can see are businesses and apartments."

"We used to sit in the schoolhouse and look out the window to the hills and trees. All you could see was the adventures that would await you as soon as school let out."

"Childhood really can be a magical time."

"It was for me. We would get out of school and walk through the trees to get home and always seemed to end up just hanging out by the creek for hours." Jodene seems to be picturing the moment as she looks out the window.

"Sounds like a lot of fun."

"It was, and I never got in trouble for being late. That was just what kids did back then. I get why everyone needs to be safe nowadays, but it is sad how much we have lost the sense of the freedom of childhood."

"I agree. Our one rule was to be home when the streetlights came on. Other than that, we had the run of the neighborhood. I remember playing hide and seek with all the kids on the street and we covered half the block for a territory."

"I tried to give my kids as much of that experience as I could, but they were raised in a different age and place than I was. It can never really be the same."

"For sure."

"Of course, now my kids are having kids, so I look forward to seeing what adventures they will be able to get into."

"That has to be a fun new stage of life."

"Oh, it's great. I get to have all the fun and spoil them but not deal with any of the responsibilities of parenting."

"Well, that's what grandparents are for."

"Of course I do wish that they could have the freedom I had as a child."

"Understandable."

"These kids will never really get the chance to know the sense of adventure and exploration the way I did growing up. They will never know what it is like to go off the path in the woods with no safety net, no fence to hold you back."

"I suppose that really is not anything that we can ever get back to."

"No, I do not think so. The closest I come to going back there is when I walk out my back door, close my eyes, and let the smell of the pine trees I planted take me back to memories of the home I remember."

"At least you have the memories you can cherish and look back to,"

"Other than my family, they are my most prized possessions."

With this last thought, we pull up to the terminal. Four lanes of cars crowd the doors in the first drop off zone. Keeping to the far left we skirt the edge of the congestion. Seeing the sign for her airline, I weave through the two left lines and into the right line where confused drivers and hurried passengers work their way through the obstacle course of cars and baggage.

"Here we are! I will get your bag out for you."

"Right at the door. Thank you!"

"Thank you so much for getting a ride. It was a pleasure to chat with you."

"You too. Have a great day."

"Thank you. Fly safe, and enjoy those trees in your back yard when you get home."

"It will be the first thing I do,"

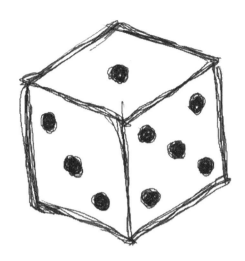

Can't Get No Satisfaction.

Twelve minutes away. That's a bit far for a standard fare. If it's a short ride, I will spend twenty minutes of my time to get three dollars. That's nine dollars per hour before taxes, not to mention gas and other expenses. Not worth it.

However, this could be an airport run that turns into over thirty bucks. Like always, it's just a gamble. Typically I wouldn't go for this one but with some personal days off planned ahead, I'm taking more trips than I normally would on a night like tonight.

My phone starts ringing. From the number, I can guess that it is most likely my passenger, Eric.

"Hello"

"You are on your way, yes?" I cannot pinpoint the accent but it is very strong, maybe Middle Eastern or African. The voice actually sounds very familiar.

"Yes, I will be there in a few minutes."

"Okay boss, I tell you where to go when you get here. You are the third driver I order and none come."

"Oh, I am sorry to hear that."

"They say they could not find me. I am right here in road waiting."

The idea that I might need to go somewhere different than is showing on the app starts to make me feel a bit uneasy.
"Okay, well I am on my way."

Twelve minutes later I am pulling down R Street to the address listed.

I drive to the place where the icon for my car lines up with the pin on the map. The address listed is not matching any of the house numbers.

I wait right there.

Nothing.

Picking up my phone again, I press redial to call Eric back.

"Okay, you are here now?"

"I am on R Street but do not see the house number you have listed."

"Drive to the end of road, you should be by school now? I am standing in road looking for you."

"What street are you on?"

"R, boss."

"R, by 43rd?"

"R, past the school, in the road. You coming to me boss?"

He speaks in a slow almost hypnotic tone, but I do not like it. His words are meant to be soothing and make me feel like his friend, but when this tone comes from a stranger luring you towards him, it creates the opposite effect.

I am in a rougher part of town, being lured to a rider that is not where they listed as the pick-up location. The words of my son echo in the back of my head again, "That's sketchy, Dad!"

Eric instructs me to make a right turn, go to the end of the road, and then make a left where the road ends. I am still in a crowded neighborhood.

"Boss, I wear yellow shirt. You see me, boss?"

Suddenly I realize why his voice sounds familiar and I can hear it in my head as a memory from a movie I recently watched. 'No problem Irish. Everything gonna be okay.' It was the voice of the leader of the Somali pirates in *Captain Phillips,* now luring me to give him a ride in my car.

"No, I am just making the last left turn." As I round the corner, Eric is impossible to miss. A scrawny spry little man, who looks like he just stepped out of a soccer game wearing a bright yellow soccer jersey with red and green soccer shorts. "I see you now."

"Good boss, you come right to me. I am here waiting." He continues guiding me down his street. "Right this way boss. Keep coming a little further." He does not end the call until after he is seated in my car. "There you are boss, perfect."

I take inventory of him as he settles into the seat. His shorts are loosely flowing enough that I can see that there is no weight in them, no objects. His hands hold only his cell phone and his body looks weak. Taking my hand off the pepper spray in my door, I reach up to start the trip.

"Heading to the casino?" It is a short trip after all of this.

"My woman won't give me the pussy!"

"Oh?"

"Yeah, so what you gonna do Boss…" Eric looks to me like this is a universal problem. "…when she won't give you the pussy?"

"Looks like you're going hunting!" I play along.

"I'm goin' the casino." He says with assurance in his decision. "I get the pussy there."

"Is the casino a good place for that?"

"Oh yeah, Boss. Lots of girls at the casino."

"Okay." I let out with a skepticism which I tried to hide. I really do not need to be convinced of where to go hunting, but am shocked by the crass commentary he is sharing about his situation and even more shocked by the ghetto-ness of his solution.

"Two years! She no give me the pussy for two years!"

"Well, I hope you find what you are looking for."

"She would not be allowed to do this back home. I from Ethiopia."

"Oh, that is cool." I hope he knows I meant where he was from, not the difference in what was tolerable. "What language do you speak in your home country?"

"Everyone in Ethiopia is bilingual. We speak Oromo and Amharic. And most speak English too."

I was happy to change the subject.

"Wow! That is really great."

"Most people do not know anything about Ethiopia. Most people think people there know nothing and only starve."

This is the second time I have been told how little we know about Africa from a passenger. The last time, I had great respect for the passenger. This guy here could do a bit more to be a better ambassador for his people.

"Here we are." Before I have time to learn more about his needs or his country, we had arrived.

"This perfect right here boss."

"Thanks for getting a ride."

"Thanks to you, boss."

"Good luck!"

I always wish people luck when leaving them at the casino. I can not help but chuckle inside at the double meaning it carries on this trip.

Backseat Driver

"Heading to the UP Library?"

"Actually going next door to Anthem Coffee."

"Nice, that's a great spot."

"Yes, I love it. And their coffee is really good too. So, do you have another job besides driving?" Tim asks one of the number one questions I get from passengers.

"Yes, I am a speaker and coach, and just do this on days when I do not have things booked."

"That is awesome man. What do you speak about?"

"Well, my main message is about accepting yourself. I have a tagline, *Own Your Awkward,* in which I challenge everyone to accept that one thing that they feel has always held them back, and make it their superpower."

"Awesome! How did you get to that message?"

"Well, I was not comfortable in my own skin and didn't accept myself for the first forty years of my life. Now that I have, I am on a mission to make sure others know just how important that is."

"That really makes sense. Where do you speak?"

"Businesses, schools or community groups typically. Since my message is all about being authentic, it relates well to leadership, sales, or just living your best life."

"How do you find your events?"

"Lots of networking. Actually driving is a great way to network too."

"For sure. I actually work with a lot of local businesses and rideshare drivers in Tacoma."

"Awesome, so you know what I mean. What kind of business do work in?"

"Well, do you have a lot of passengers that ask where to go or what there is to do in town?"

"Yes, every day."

"Well. I have designed an app that lists all the great local hot spots in one place, so they can get recommendations from locals." Tim holds up his phone so I can see the app opening up.

"That sounds like a really great idea. I will have to check it out."

"It's called BD Local, the BD stands for Backseat Driver. We actually mount iPads in the back of rideshare drivers' cars so the passengers can look through local hot spots while you drive. They can also download the app on their phone."

"Awesome."

"If you have a second, I can show you when we stop."

"For sure."

Pulling in front of the entrance on the back side of the mall I park and look back to check out Tim's phone.

"See here are the different sections. *Shop local* has deals you can take advantage of at local businesses. *Twenty One Plus Activities* will tell you about the bars and weed shops. And then we have *Kid's Stuff*, and *What's Hot*. That is where we list local artists and musicians. Passengers can listen to local music and podcasts right here in the app while they ride along."

"Wow! That is really a cool idea. Looks like you have some of the best hot spots in there already."

"Yes, here is my card in case you want to let us know of your favorite spots that we should add, or if you wanna see about getting set up with an iPad in your car."

"Thanks, I know of a bunch that should be in there. Here is my card as well."

"Thanks for the ride. Drive safe."

"Thanks, have a great day."

Two Kids and One Arm

It is a simple text message: *I'm wearing a long pink dress standing by the mailboxes.*

Thank you. I will be right there. This is how so many of my new relationships start. Don't get too worried they are typically only five-minute relationships anyway.

"Hi there, Jaymi right? I'm sorry the GPS had me on the other side of your complex."

"Yes, that's me. You're fine. I don't know if I want to go anyway, but I already paid the babysitter."

Now that I have started the trip I can see her destination. We are going to the Loose Wheel Bar & Grill. "No worries, It's always good to get away for a night out. Going to the Loose Wheel?"

"Yes, I have never been there before."

"It is a fun spot."

"I am just not sure about this guy?"

"Oh? Is this a first date?"

The Loose Wheel does not seem like it would be my choice for a first date hot spot, but everyone has different tastes and favorites.

I can say they make a killer club sandwich and their wings are the talk of the town. The last time I was there, my friend mixed their Stupid Sauce (so named for being so hot you would be stupid to try it) into my ketchup. So in dunking a tot full on into the trap, my mouth was on fire. Painful as it was the memories of this place are good and always fun.

She may have a way better first date than I would have in the safety of a quiet restaurant or coffee shop, checking items off the *getting to know you* list.

"Yes, I met him online."

"That is cool."

"He sent me a picture of a wad of cash so I am not sure what he is expecting."

"I have not done much with the online dating thing, but that seems odd to me."

"Yeah, maybe he was offering to pay for babysitting, but he did not say that. It is better than most of the pictures I have sent to me."

"Really?" I do not have to think much on it to imagine what she is referring to.

"What is it with guys thinking we need to see their genitalia?"

"I do not know, I guess you do not have to worry about any surprises." I try to keep the conversation as light as possible.

"I do not date much. It is hard to find a guy open to my situation. I have two kids and my arm so I weed out a lot of guys."

I am not sure I understand what she means, or if I heard her right, but I can understand that dating with kids is an added dynamic. "Well, maybe you will at least have a fun night out, even if he is not the one for you."

"I like your tunes" as the melody of *American Pie* starts to fill the car. "It's karaoke night so we are going to have to warm up!" and out belts her version of the song. "…drove my Chevy to the levee but the levee was dry…"

"Alright." As I pump the volume up a bit and let her do her thing. She is not half bad, a little timid which is understandable but she is holding her own.

"…and the three men I admire most…" The song comes to an end and the next tune starts up, *Stand By Me.*

"When the night has come, and the land is dark…"
She starts up and then abruptly stops and looks unhappily towards me. "Come on! You are supposed to be backing me up!"

"Huh? Me sing?" People expect way too much out of their rideshare drivers.

"Yeah! I said *we* were going to warm up." Jaymi pursues

"Oh, I thought you meant *you* needed the warm-up for your date."

"Come on, sing!"

"I am no good, in fact, I have been told to not sing in public."

"So you are going to let me just sing alone?"

"Fine, but no promises on quality or refunds for being off tune."

"Deal"

"Here goes nothing." I think to myself as I try to sing along. It feels like that awkward moment when they bring cake into the break room at work and no one wants to get into the singing enough to really sing well. I am off key, mess up the lyrics and almost miss a turn.

As the chorus comes I figure I should just go for it. I start to belt it out, still out of key, but just singing the way I do when I am cruising down the freeway alone with the volume all the way up.

"So darling, darling
Stand by me, oh stand by me
Oh stand, stand by me
Stand by me"

Letting go of your inhibitions is not easy, but once done, you can find yourself connecting in a way that is relaxed and natural. There is something about being vulnerable with another person that drives a natural connection.

We both laugh as the song moves along and I am faced with the sudden realization of how many of the lyrics I actually do not know, or at least do not know when they are supposed to be sung.

Jaymi seems to know the song really well and she does not let my bad timing and off-key belting detour her from her course.

By the time the song is over, we are pulling up to The Loose Wheel.

Using her left arm to reach across herself to open the door, I notice for the first time that her right arm is a prosthetic. Now I understand what she was saying earlier about dating with kids and her arm. She is fun and very nice so, whether the money wad guy is right for her or not, I have no doubt she will find a good match to sing along with soon enough.

"Thanks for getting a ride, and good luck tonight!"

"Thank you, it was a fun ride!"

Suddenly I have a craving for a club sandwich with a side of tots, but following her inside would just be awkward. I let the craving go for another day and end the trip and prepare for whatever may be in store on the next ride.

Oink Oink

It's nights like this when I wonder what I am doing with my life. The silence between rides, the monotony of finding busy work, or inevitable boredom from the attempts to entertain myself while waiting for a call, can all become a bit depressing.

This lot is at least busy enough to provide some people watching as shoppers hustle in and out of the busy Stadium Thriftway. My biggest struggle right now is resisting the urge to go inside and grab myself a cookie from the bakery.

I have learned that it is better to wait in busy parking lots, surrounded by people and full of life than to be the only car in an empty lot after all of the businesses have closed for the night. At least in a full lot, I can blend in with life and feel like part of a community.

It has been twenty minutes since my last ride. My head is doing simple math as my hourly rate decreases with every minute that passes. At some point, I will need to decide if I am going to stay out later just to get to the number I need, or give up and hope to drive in busier times another day.

Finally, my phone lights up: *Pick up Justin.*

He is not too far away. I can be there in about seven minutes. I would have taken a ride at this point even if it was further, but this is at least closer to what I would take anyway.

Seven minutes later I am parked in front of a 1960's style rambler with all the signs of being a family home: a kid's bike leaned up against the garage, a soccer ball that seems to have rolled under the front shrub to stay hidden since their last impromptu match, and what appears to be some homemade art hanging on the front porch.

"How are you tonight? Justin, right?"

"Yes, man. I am great. How are you?"

"I am well thanks."

"Sweet. Just heading over to hang out with a friend for a couple of hours and figured I might as well get a ride in case we have a drink."

"Good plan! Always better to plan ahead just in case."

"I do not know his address, but he is right across the street from Shake Shake Shake."

"Shake Shake Shake?"

"Do you not know where that is?"

"No. Sorry."

"It is right in the middle of the Stadium District."

"I was just over there and I know the area really well. I just can't picture that."

"Oh dude, you have to go to Shake Shake Shake. Best burgers and shakes ever."

"I believe you."

"Are you from Tacoma?"

"Yes, I grew up here."

"And you haven't been to Shake Shake Shake?"

"No, but I am getting caught up on a lot of stuff lately."

"Well, I am going to show you where it is for sure."

"Sounds great."

"I'd go there right now myself, but I have been promising my friend that I would get over there so we could practice and try some new songs out."

"Oh cool, like singing or what?"

"Ya, I am very musical. We write music and I even have a band with my kids."

"That is pretty cool. I am sure they love doing music with their dad. What type of music do you guys play?"

"Rock."

"Fun. So how does that work? Do you just kinda play what you want and give them small parts to join in?"

"No, they play drums and guitar and sing most of the vocals. They also write a lot of the songs, or we write them together."

"Wow! That is really impressive. So is this like a *School of Rock* thing?"

"I guess you could say that. You can hear some of our songs online if you want."

"Awesome! What is your band called?" I did not think this to be too intrusive to ask, but Justin seems to shy up a bit before he answers.

"We are called Pig Snout."

"Pig Snout?"

"Yeah, you know, like the nose of a pig."

"Yeah, I get it. Cool name."

"Well, my kid's named the band."

"Haha, even better!"

"See, right there, that is Shake Shake Shake."

"Oh, duh! Yeah, I know this place. I have not tried them out yet, but it looks like such an awesome place."

I cannot tell you how many times I have driven by this restaurant. It has the look of the classic American fifties diner complete with stools wrapping around a bar style counter where they make your shakes. Three giant lighted letters on the back wall can be seen from a block away that spell out EAT.

"You really gotta try it soon."

"I will for sure. So do you guys ever play at any gigs around town?"

"Yes. We have played at Jazzbones, at Wright park this summer, and have some stuff coming up soon."

"Awesome. I will look you up and try to get to something.

TMI

As Brianna approaches the car, her welcoming smile lets me know that she will be a pleasant rider. The fact that it is leaves me to figure this will be a pretty typical ride. As she settles in, I ready for the usual questions and for the discussion to go from there.

"Heading to The Loose Wheel?"

"Yes, thanks. I am meeting a friend."

"Well, that is a fun place for that."

Our ride starts out just as I expect: the big three. Do you do rideshare full time? What do you do in your off time? Well actually, we never make it to three. The first two turn the course of the conversation and from there, I am now in driving and listening mode.

"I drive part-time as a rideshare driver, but I am a motivational speaker and really aspire to be a writer."

"You mean you *already are* a writer, you just aspire to be published."

"True that!"

"I started writing for a blog." She shares as she pulls out her phone. As of yet, I had not noticed her to be in any compromised state.

"Online dating, and bad decisions!" she announces as she starts to read from her mobile device.

"This gets a little personal" she interposes through the side of her lips while peering around from behind her phone as if using it to hide her shyness.

"Let's not mince words, I am obese, not chubby, not overweight, but obese. But I still get fucked. Men have their fetishes, and I am chased and fucked, not made love to, but fucked."

"Wow, this *is* personal." I think to myself. She was right about that and she isn't holding back.

We merge onto the freeway to start the jaunt across town as Brianna continues on.

"I meet men online, it is just easier. Easier to weed out the creeps and losers, and takes less time and effort than going out in public to any random place to deal with every guy that may approach. From time to time I even find a guy worth dating and then have to explain to them why I am not on the pill: that I do not feel the need to add hormones to my body every day just in case some guy wants to get off and does not feel comfortable with a condom on."

Not to mention all the diseases being shared comes to mind. But before I have time to really finish the thought we are on to the next level already.

"Then eventually it happens, one comes along that seems like he may be worth seeing more than just that one night stand. So as it happens, I find myself at the doctor after two weeks of knowing him to discuss birth control options. The pill is not the best for me and at my size, the doc recommends against a shot so we settle on the NuvaRing."

Just to be clear to the audience, I have no idea what this thing is. But I do not ask, I let Brianna continue on, uninterrupted in her story. One thing that I can appreciate, regardless of subject matter, is that no matter what your story is, people appreciate being heard, and a writer always appreciates an audience to listen to their story.

"So home I head to prepare for my next Saturday night date. It's time for me to insert the ring"

Okay, so at this point, I believe that I am starting to get a guess as to what this 'ring' may be, and where it may need to go.

"No matter how many yoga style moves I try to do, I can not reach down, around, and back up to get to my cervix."

Really now, I know what that is, and where it is and now I have a very clear picture. Yes, this story does get personal.

Brianna continues on. "After two hours of stretching, pulling, reaching and sweating, I give up, clean up, shower, and head over to my new man's house. I arrive, somewhat put together with a bent ring in my hand, and a look of defeat on my face. He could reach what I could not and managed to secure the ring over my cervix and now we could enjoy condom-free sex. That is of course, for the next two weeks until we broke up. And now here I was two weeks later without a man, but with a ring over my cervix that I cannot reach."

"How far out are we?" I wonder to myself. GPS says that we are about 8 minutes away from the bar. I am wondering where we are in the timeline of the story. Did she break up last night? Is that thing still in there? What is happening right now on my passenger seat? What is she expecting to get out of this rideshare ride?

"I tried again to assume the yoga poses necessary to free myself from the ring but it was a fruitless endeavor. Not wanting to see my doctor to ask for help nor to pay a $35 co-pay just to have her reach further than I can, I called a good friend. She and I had been intimate before and I knew I could count on her to help."

Whoa! What kind of friend is that? And just in case any of my friends may read this, that is an off-limits request!

"So after another intimate moment with my friend, a bottle of wine and a pizza, we were back to a girl's night, without men or the need for birth control"

"Well," I start. "You are a talented writer and tell a good story."

"Thanks, I am a little drunk already." She says as we pull into the parking lot.

"You know last time I dropped someone off here she was going on a date with a guy she met online. She had to practice karaoke the whole ride there to warm up."

"I have never been here before, but I am meeting a guy here."

"Oh, is this a new date?" thinking maybe it's the same guy and this is his regular first date spot.

"No, we've met a couple of weeks ago. We've fucked a couple of times." She explains in a casual way as if to say it's all cool. And with that last comment, the passenger door closes and on she went with the adventures of her life.

Genevieve the Bouncer

The Orion, you can't miss it. It is a big white block of apartments on the block that transitions from downtown to the Stadium district. I am not sure the year it was built but the plain simple lines leave to the imagination that it could have just dropped in place any day in the last fifty years and already seemed both modern and outdated at the same time.

Pulling into the loading zone I click the alert to let Genevieve know I have arrived.

Letting go of an embrace with a man, she heads from the entrance towards me. Her personality makes its way into the car well before she does. Her walk seems to have a bounce in it like Tigger on the way to a new adventure. Though she does not have a tail with a spring in it, she does carry a head full of red corkscrew locks which seem to lift her up with each stride.

"Hi, Genevieve right?"

"Yes! How *are* you today?"

"I am great. How are you?"

"Excellent! I just need to head back to my house in Lakewood."

I have gotten used to the idea by now, that even when I pick someone up from a home or apartment, it may not necessarily be where they live. So many folks use a rideshare to visit friends, family, partners, or even just hookups.
Heading back towards downtown to get on the highway, Genevieve spots The Grand Cinema. "Have you been to The Grand?"

"No, I still need to do that. It is definitely on my list. It looks like such a cool little theater."

"Oh, you *have* to try it!" She has a way of accentuating words in almost every sentence, but not in an annoying valley girl way, more in a zest for life that she just *has* to share with others way. "The people there are *so* friendly and they always have some *really* unique indie films showing."

"That is what I have noticed. Every time I see an event pop up, the films are usually shows I have never heard of and they seem to have a very wide variety in interests and topics."

"Yes, one week it could be a documentary on the way a world leader changed history, the next week it could be an artsy drama made by an independent filmmaker. And then they might just have an entire show that is a compilation of YouTube cat videos."

"I actually dropped someone off a couple weeks ago who was going to watch the cat video movie."

"Oh, it was actually really *good*. My boyfriend and I saw that one. We were not sure what to expect, but it was amazing."

"Who thinks of making a movie just out of cat videos?"

"I know right!" She was on a mission now to make sure I had this experience soon. "Here's what you do, you get there early and go next door to Corina bakery first. Have you tried *them* yet?"

"No. They are also on my list to try too. There are just so many great places to get to around here."

"Oh for sure." She does not lose a beat in her excitement. "Go to Corina and order their banana pudding and a coffee. Then you take it into the theater with you. They let you bring in *outside* food to enjoy during the movie. That is the *perfect* combination."

"That sounds really good."

"Even if you don't really like banana, which is not my favorite. The way they make this is to *die* for." It is the first time she actually uttered the words 'to die for' during the ride, but I felt that her zest for life suggested them with everything she mentioned.

"Well…" As I start to reply my words are interrupted by the sound of her phone ringing.

"Hey there."

Pause.

"Oh no, are you still at home?"

She goes on with a conversation I hear only half of, but my Holmes' abilities tell me that someone is at home with a car that does not run.

"That was my daughter and her car is not starting. She has to get to work so I guess she will be taking a rideshare as well. How would that work if I wanted her to use you?"

"Oh well, it's pretty easy. Is she at the address we are heading to?"

"Yes, she is at home, fortunately."

"Well, she can either wait 'til I am in front of the house to order the ride, at which point it should go to me as the closest driver, or you can just leave this fare going and we can update the final drop off location. However, you prefer."

"Is that a pain for you to have to wait if it takes her a minute to get out the door?"

"Nah, it does not matter to me. I would just be finding a place to park and wait for my next ride either way."

"Cool, you're the best. I am going to text her right now and let her know to just sit tight 'til we get there"

We are close now and the conversation carries on about other things around the city as well as Genevieve's curiosity about who I am, other than a rideshare driver.

That is always in the top two questions that I am asked. It is always 'what else do you do', and 'what are your craziest stories'. Genevieve's spiral curls carry the same life that her personality does as she bounces from topic to topic with curiosity and excitement the entire ride.

Pulling up to the small craftsman home with a picket fence she gathers her bag and heads in to send Amelia out to get to work.

Amelia is pleasant but not chatty as her mom was. It is not quite an elevator ride but close to it.

"Have a great day. I hope your car is not hard or expensive to fix." I leave her with, as she heads into work.

"Thanks, I am glad you were around at the right time!"

"Thanks!"

It has been a good ride, experiencing the light Genevieve brings to the world, followed by the chance to get someone to work who needed a ride. This is what makes driving meaningful.

I know you!

It starts like any normal trip. A little after one am, bars thinning out as I show up to find two guys and a gal waiting under the glow of the sign at Crown Bar.

"Looks like we're going to Lakewood?"

"Yeah, that's right."

I start to drive the right direction while the GPS catches up to where we are, and in which direction we are heading.

About a half mile down the road it starts to get really weird.

"Dude, I know you!" Spouts out of the scruffy drunk from the back seat.

"Really?"

"Yeah man, you don't remember me?"

"Sorry but it's hard to tell through the rearview mirror."

"I know you man!"

"Brandon, you do not know the rideshare guy!" Chimes in the wife.

"I know him! Seriously, I know him"

"Just ignore him, he had a bit to drink tonight" adds the clean-cut less drunk from the front seat.

"It's all good, I have seen all sorts." I reassure the group.

"I really do know you! Dude! You don't remember me?" Drunk people can take things so personally.

"Sorry man."

"Dude!"

"Brandon! Chill" she pushes.

"But I know him!"

"No, ya don't!"

"Didn't you work like in a grocery store or something?"

So admittedly now this is starting to get weird. How would the scruffy drunk know that?

"Yes, actually. But that was a long time ago."

"See I told you. How would I know that?"

"Okay, so were you a customer?"

"Nah dude, you don't remember me?"

"Just drawing a blank man. Sorry."

"Dude, I walk with your wife"

"Seriously Brandon! Cut it out. You have gone too far!" She is really agitated now. I can only guess that adding in another woman is enough to push her over the top.

"You walk with my wife?"

"Yeah, I walk with your wife."

"Brandon, dude, leave it alone." Clean cut, less drunk is trying to help from the front seat.

"At graduation, I walked with your wife."

"Oh seriously? Walked? I thought you said walk, as in you go walking with her now." Now, this all makes sense. "Brandon, gotcha! I did not recognize you with the beard."

"Isn't that what people say, they walked?"

"I suppose, it's just been twenty-three years and didn't really have high school on my mind."

"See, I told you I knew the rideshare guy!"

"Okay seriously Brandon, you can cut it out now."

I do not get the feeling that him being right, makes his wife feel any better.

"Looks like we are here." The timing of the ride saves me from getting into the story of us having just split up. "I will tell her I saw you."

"Totally! Thanks for the ride man."

"Thanks for getting one. See you around!"

Maybe I should have told them my story. As annoying as Brandon was, his brother was cute. Just one more ride that I will always wonder about.

Apples

"Just heading back home."

Bob settles into the car quickly after walking down the long walk from a Craftsman style home in a quiet residential part of Old Town Tacoma.

"Okay. Sounds great."

"The GPS never gets it right so I will show you where to go when we get close."

"Sounds good. That can happen a lot in some neighborhoods."

"Yeah, for some reason it doesn't recognize our street and so it always takes you to the neighborhood behind ours."

"That won't work then."

"Right? I am not gonna hop fences just to get home."

"I am sure your neighbors appreciate that too."

"Besides, I can't afford a sprained ankle tomorrow. I gotta get up and be ready to hit it early in the morning."

"Oh, are you going to hit the Black Friday specials?"

"No, no, no. It's the Apple Cup and I am getting up early to make the drive to Pullman."

The Apple Cup is the big rivalry football game between the state's two biggest universities, UW, or the Huskies, and WSU or the Cougars. The game is usually the day after Thanksgiving and alternates which school hosts each year.

This year the game is at WSU in Pullman, a good five and a half hours from Tacoma in good conditions. Having to cross the Cascade Mountains, then drive another couple hours through farm country in Eastern Washington, you never know how the weather may be this time of year.

"That is awesome. That should be a fun game. You are obviously a Cougar." Bob's crimson hat and sweatshirt left no question as to who he would be rooting for in tomorrow's game.

"Yes! For sure. And I never miss an Apple Cup."

"Nice! It is a fun game to watch." I do not honestly watch many sports, but I have enjoyed a few games over the years so it is not a complete lie.

"So who's your team?"

"Honestly, I have never really been partial to either. However, this is my son's first year at Wazzu so I actually have a good reason to want the Cougs to win."

"Sweet. My Dad and Grandpa both went to Wazzu so I grew up watching the Apple Cup with them. We went to a few of the games when I was a kid and before my grandpa died we started going to all of the games together. Well until he got too sick to travel and go out."

"That is such a great thing to have been able to share together."

"Yes, that is why I will never miss an Apple Cup. I promised myself when my grandpa died, that I would go to every Apple Cup to honor and remember him."

"Wow. That is quite a commitment. But a beautiful way to continue to celebrate his life."

"It's been eight years, and I have not missed any yet. Oh, don't turn here. Go straight and turn at the stop sign."

"Gotcha. Thanks for catching that. That really is a beautiful story. Sports mean so much more than just the games and stats."

"Yes, it is how we stayed together as a family, even through some pretty rough shit."

"I am glad to hear that you got through it."

"Yeah, and Grandpa really was the one who kept the whole family together through it all."

"I can see why it means so much to carry on this tradition then."

"Yes, for sure. It is more than just a memory from my childhood. It is about honoring everything he did for all of us."

"That is really awesome."

"Oh turn down the next street. Then it's the second house on the right."

"This one here?"

"Yes."

"I could guess from the Cougar flag."

"You know it!"

"Thanks for getting a ride! And drive careful tomorrow."

"Thanks. You too!"

Even though the next day would bring a snowy defeat on the field for the Cougars, I know it was a win for Bob as he made his way across the state to honor the grandfather who did so much for him and his family.

Jim & Barbara

They are the perfect looking couple. Of course, by perfect I mean in looks only.

If you are a fan of *Gotham,* then you will know what I mean when I say that this is Jim Gordon and Barbara to every last detail. A suited up young man with a confidence and stride that carry him while being yoked by a blonde woman who is hot to the point of showing a very dangerous level on the hot-crazy scale.

The pair walk out of the club with the clashing themes of confidence and defeat as they approach the car. Alma Mater has quickly become the hot spot in town for concerts and other events. Barbara walks at a faster pace and does not hesitate to claim the front seat leaving Jim to have the full use of the back.

"Hi there, thanks for getting a ride." My standard greeting rolls out. "Heading over to University Place?"

"Yes, we are staying at my parents' place while we visit." Jim shares from behind my ear.

"That's cool. I usually try not to pry too much."

"Well, you could just stop talking like he does."

Not sure if she is just slamming him, or if she really wants me to shut the hell up, I err on the side of a quieter ride and let the music be the only sound to fill the car.

"Where are you going?" She seems to disagree with the route.

"Just heading up to Sprague to cut over to Highway 16."

"His GPS will take the best route."

"Whatever." She blows him off.

"Do you have any better music?"

Barbara doesn't wait for an answer as she reaches over to change the station. I am on my *Driving Ditties* playlist running through the AUX chord, so any buttons she touches really does not make a change. But to be accommodating I switch it to radio mode so she can find what she likes. She finds a rock song and leans back in her chair only after cranking it up just a bit more.

Glad that is done. Maybe she is settled in and comfortable now.

Though the music blares, the car holds a kind of heavy silence that carries us down the dark roads.

This is when I feel it start to happen. If it was meant to be soft and subtle, she failed. The potions from the club had taken that skill from her hours ago.

My knee is the first to feel her touch. A full open hand with the palm touching down first on my knee cap, then the fingers fall down around the rest of my leg and over my joint like a blanket falling into place over the top of a red rubber ball.

Had it been Jim, my heart would stir. It is her though. I could close my eyes and pretend, but I am in the driver's seat. What is she doing? He's gonna kick my ass if he sees this.
Her grip loosens as her talon moves up the side of my leg. I slide my right arm down to block any progress, literally a cock block.

Pulling her arm from my outer thigh, she redeploys her forces and tries for an aerial attack. Now coming from above and straight to the inner thigh.

This would be arousing were it at a slower pace and with the stronger hairier hands of Jim. Launching my own surface to air defense system, I shift my arm to create a barrier between her attack and the key to the city.

She is leaning in with full force now. Is Jim awake? Did he pass out? Is he gonna kick my ass? What should I do? Shifting my body weight away from the threat, I race through the options in my head. Her troops regroup for one more assault as I put up a full hard stop with my forearm.

It's now that I hear the tap of a hand on her right shoulder. It's Jim. He is awake and calling off the forces.

"I am sorry honey, I love you so much" leaves her lips as she shifts her weight back to the opposite side of the car away from me.

These were the last words spoken for the remainder of the trip as we drive along in an even heavier silence than before.

Like so many of my trips, I doubt I will ever see Jim and Barbara again.

Again

Pull around to the side, I will be right out. It seems a bit eerie that they know where I am and send a message through the phone. That is after all how these apps are designed to work, but it feels like I am being watched and cannot see by whom.

Seeing Tim come out of the house I feel a bit better knowing he is a repeat passenger.

"Hey there, thanks for getting a ride again."

"Hey man, good to see you. Thanks for picking me up."

I have a memory for people and this is the second ride I have given Tim. He's the guy with the BD Local app to highlight local businesses in the back of rideshare cars.

"How is it going with your app?"

"It's going really well. We keep getting more businesses on board every day."

"That is sweet, I did download the app and have checked it out a couple of times but still need to click on the *Share Local* button to send you some of my favorites."

"All good my friend. How are things with your business?"

"Good, I started doing a podcast. It's called *Own Your Awkward,* and each week I have a different guest on to share something awkward that they have had to get over or own in order to get to where they are today."

"Nice, how is that going?"

"So far so good, I have done my first three episodes, but I am already booked up for the next two months."

"Sweet. I will have to check it out."

"Please do. Looks like we are here already."

"Anywhere over here is good. The entrance is down that ramp."

"Thanks for getting a ride again. I will send you some locations soon."

"That would be great. Thanks. Have an awesome day."

"You too."

It's always great to see a repeat passenger, especially the friendly ones. Who knows if I will see Tim again, but I will at least send him some of my favorite spots around town to get added to his app.

Weed Walmart Repeat

Pick up Eli flashes across my screen.

Eli is in Ruston, a quaint little town that is bordered by Tacoma on two sides and the Puget Sound on the other. There are two Mayberry-like towns nestled along the edges of Tacoma: Fircrest and Ruston.

Pushing the notification to let Eli know I have arrived, I settle in and wait for him to make it out the door.

This can be awkward as I sit in front of someone's home watching for signs of life. Just often enough the passenger does not catch that the address picked up by the rideshare app is across the street or a couple of houses down the road.

For this reason, I do not pull into the driveway to wait but stay on the street, where I can easily pull forward, and also not freak out anyone who is not expecting a car to be sitting in their driveway.

Finally, I see the door slide open and a young hoody and jeans guy makes his way to the car.

"Heading over to the rec shop?" I learned previously that with the changing of the laws in Washington, weed shops are no longer called dispensaries. This was a term reserved for the sale of medical marijuana and as it is now legal for recreational use, all outlets are now considered recreational marijuana shops.

"Yes."

"Sounds good."

"Can you tell me when this gets to thirty dollars?"

"Well, the rideshare app doesn't show me what the rate is tracking along the ride, but it should have given you a fare estimate when you ordered the ride."

"Oh okay."

"I wouldn't think that a ride across town would be close to thirty bucks. But there are several closer shops between the one you entered and here."

"Oh I know, but this one has a specific kinda thing I am looking for. Have you ever heard of moon rock?"

"No, what's that?"

"It's like getting the dust from the processing and having it rolled into wax to create this really potent hit. It is hard to find and can be pretty expensive. This place has some for fifteen bucks and everywhere else it would be like forty."

"Wow! Sounds like a pretty good deal."

It takes about fifteen minutes to get from Ruston to Parkland to make it to the Gallery where Eli could get the deal on his special weed.

"Can you wait for me to get what I need and then take me back home?"

"Yes, I can. Do you want to just leave the ride running? If I end it and you reorder, I may end up getting a trip while you are in there."

"Yeah, just leave it and I will be quick."

Pot shop stops usually do not take too long, especially with the experienced shoppers. They typically know exactly what they need and it is just a matter of telling the budtender their order.

A few minutes later, Eli makes his way back out. "This was the wrong shop."

"Oh no, is it in the system wrong? This is where the GPS was programmed for."

"No, I mean, I put in the wrong shop. I called two or three, but then put the wrong address in the app. But it turned out alright because they had a different variety here that I wanted to try out."

"Well, that's good at least. So do you want to go to the other shop still?"

"Yes, I will change the address. It's called Mary Mart" As I wait he adds, "Actually I need to go to Walmart to get a money order."

"Okay, well Mary Mart is back closer to where you live and Walmart is on the way there."

"Oh I don't live there, I am just staying with family while I get settled here."

"Cool."

It's the same routine when we get to Walmart, he runs in to get his money order while I hover in the lot waiting for his return. He leaves a bag of weed in my car so I know he will be back.

"They were not open."

"Oh no! Was the store closing up?"

"No, just the money order counter is closed for the day."

"Oh, gotcha. Do you still want to go to Mary Mart?"

"Yes, let's head over there."

"Okay, should be there in just a couple minutes." Sure enough, we arrive in no time. Having made it across town from Ruston to Parkland with a stop back through Central Tacoma, we were now at Mary Mart and just a couple miles away from Ruston again.

While Eli heads in to search out his deal on moonrock, I check in on my messages and have time to send a couple of replies. He is not a bad guy, but I am ready for this trip to be over.

"Glad they still had them." Eli lets out as he takes the passenger seat again. "There is supposed to be another Walmart in Lakewood that still has the money order counter open, can we head over there."

"Works for me. Wish we knew earlier because that was on the way back from Parkland and we would not have needed to backtrack." It really does not make a difference to me, I just feel bad that he is racking up a bill.

"It's all good."

Finally making it out of the second Walmart with a money order in hand, Eli lets me know that he is ready to head back to Ruston.

"Do you ever smoke?"

"Nah, not really. I have a couple of times but I am not a good smoker."

"Mind if I roll a blunt in your car? I do not like to do it back at the place I am staying with family around."

"I don't care." Eli pulls the weed out from his first bag as well as a box of Swisher Sweets. "Are you going to smoke those at the same time you smoke your joint?"

"Nah, it's going to be a blunt. I'll show you. Blunts are rolled in tobacco and not regular paper like joints."

Pulling out one of the Swishers, be cuts it down the side and begins to scrape the tobacco into the small white paper bag which had just been emptied of its contents.

"I never knew the difference. And I have never seen anyone do it like that."

"It's the best way, the tobacco leaf mixed with the weed is amazing. You want to try it with me?"

"Nah, I am good. I would just end up coughing so much."

"You sure, we could go to the park and smoke or something." Eli seems to be a master at making blunts as he carefully balances the dissected Swisher on his knee while crumbling bits of weed into the center cavity.

"I am good, but thanks for the offer." As I watch Eli use his spit as an adhesive to close the blunt back up, I cannot imagine putting that in my mouth, even if I was the least bit curious. "Looks like we are here."

"Alright, if you are sure you don't wanna go smoke with me?"

"Sorry bud, I gotta keep working. Thanks for getting a ride and for the education though."

"Sure thing. Thanks for taking me around."

Eli slowly walks back to the house that isn't his home with a money order in one hand and two bags of weed in the other. I wonder where he will find to smoke away from family, and if he will find a smoking buddy to take with him as I pull away towards my next ride.

To Die For

Pick up Genevieve displays on my phone as I pull up to O'Malleys.

O'Malley's is one of Tacoma's great Irish pubs, and a fun one at that. The last time I was here was to celebrate my niece turning twenty-one. I hate to say that I found selfies on my phone the next day with people I do not even know. The last thing I remember from that night was my nephew making sure I was getting into the right rideshare to get home.

As I search for clarity in those memories, I see a head of hair and a personality leaping towards my car and I immediately recognize her as Genevieve, the bouncer. At least that is the nickname I gave her.

"Hi, great to see you again. Going back to the Orion?" She is with the man from her goodbye embrace when I picked her up previously. I had caught on last time to the idea that the Orion is his place. "I gave you a ride home when your daughter also needed a ride to work a couple of months ago."

"I was thinking you looked *really* familiar." Yep, definitely her, with the same accentuations along for the ride as well.

"How have you been?"

"*Great!* We were just out for a night painting the town red."

"That sounds like a lot of fun."

"Well, you really *can't beat* the nightlife on Sixth Ave."

"Yes, it is one of my favorite parts of town."

"We started at The Red Hot for one of their really *tasty* hot dogs and then worked our way down the strip."

"They have an awesome menu. You know, I still haven't made it to Corina Bakery to try their banana pudding yet."

"Well, you absolutely *must!* You know it's to die for."

"It is definitely on my list."

In the five-minute drive along Sixth Avenue toward their building, we banter back and forth a bit more. I assure her that I will make it to Corina and The Grand Cinema very soon.

Then before we know it the ride comes to an end.

"Have a great night! Thanks for getting a ride again!"

"You too! Have an *amazing* evening!"

And out of my life walks Genevieve, the bouncer forever.

Race

"Hi there, who are you here to pick up?"

His sly smile tells me that this is nothing more than a witty and charming play to snag the first car to show up.

"I'm sorry but you really don't have the look of a Jennifer." I replied with a smile.

"I could be Jennifer." He replies and then pushes. "What if Jennifer doesn't show up, then can I get in?"

"Sure, but I have to give her a chance to get here first."

"Jennifer! Jennifer!" The man starts shouting through the crowd standing outside The Stone.

Short for The Silverstone, The Stone is a gay bar which evolves into a club on Friday and Saturday nights when the back room fills up with people from every walk of life hitting the dance floor.

"Doesn't look like she's coming. I don't see a Jennifer anywhere."

"Sorry man it looks like she's around back. I just got a text from her."

"Dang!"

"Nice try though."

Pulling around the block I find two couples.

"Jennifer, right?"

"We love your music!" As *Yakety Sax* plays through the speakers. "And yes, I'm Jennifer. We would be stoked if you can beat my jackass husband and drunk brother-in-law home!"

Just the ladies get in the car and the guys hop into a jeep parked right behind where they were all waiting.

The destination loads in my app and I see it is just a short trip, less than a mile up the hill and down the road.

Turning the music up a bit more, I pull around the corner and stop at the light at the bottom of the hill in downtown. Before us lay a series of red traffic lights acting as gatekeepers up the steep hill of downtown Tacoma.

As the song ends, I start to wonder what the next song will be. My playlist covers many genres and decades so it could turn to anything from something zany and fun, to something slower. I was glad to hear a fun song start as *Come on Eileen* starts its instrumental opening.

"Love your music! Can you turn it up more?"

"Of course. I usually have it on full blast. So how high do you want me to go?"

"As loud as you can handle."

As if on command the lights before us turn from red to green. It feels like an urban parting of the Red Sea as the open road lay ahead.

Turning the volume to full blast while I simultaneously floor it, we start to fly up the hill of downtown. As the road flattens out at each intersection, it feels like we are actually getting air between the tires and the ground.

Laughter erupts in the back seat. I can feel the laughter in the car, but I cannot hear anything other than the music blaring through the speakers.

Reaching the top of the hill I feel a pat on my shoulder.

"Turn here! Turn here!" Screams from the back seat.

Making the hard fast turn just in time, I am met with more screams.

"Oh no! Not that one, the next one!"

"I will pull around."

"Damnit! They are going to beat us home now."

This is one of those blocks that has such a narrow road, only one car at a time can slide between the rows of parked cars on each side. I feel like Luke flying through the narrow passages inside of the Death Star.

I should mention, it feels like we are going much faster than we actually are. The quick acceleration, the dips in the hills, and the loud music all mess with our senses.

A hard left, another hard left, another long block of narrow road, and we are coming up to their home.

"This one! This one!"

"Right at the end?"

"Yes! Yes! And they are not back yet!"

Jennifer and her friend start high-fiving in the back seat as we come to a fast stop at the end of their walkway.

"You have to run inside and act like you have been here for a while already."

"Yes, c'mon. Let's hurry."

Laughing and hollering as they race up the walk to the porch, they yell back:

"Best rideshare ever!"

My work here is done. On to the next ride for the night.

Snow

Stadium High School is one of the coolest schools in the country, speaking architecturally at least. Pulling up to Stadium, you would think you have transported yourself back in time to a European castle.

Originally designed in the late eighteen hundreds as a fancy hotel, it was built to resemble a French chateau. The hotel would never open, but now the school sits in its place balancing on a hillside, and towering above the water, overlooking the Puget Sound and the Cascade foothills. If you have seen the movie *Ten Things I Hate About You,* then you have seen Stadium High School. Some people call it America's Hogwarts.

Pulling up to the school I see a lone student walking my way from the brick courtyard.

"Andy, right?"

"Yes. Ken? How are you today?"

"Correct. I am good. I am still getting used to it here."

"Here at Stadium?"

"Washington."

"Oh, how do you like it so far?"

"It is cold, but I like it."

"So where are you from?"

"The Philippines."

"Oh, that is a long ways away. I have never been but I imagine it is much warmer there than it is here."

"Yes very much so. I am getting used to the cold. I am really looking forward to seeing snow. When does the snow come?" Hope and excitement fill Ken's eyes.

"Oh, it is hard to tell. Some years it does not snow at all." The hope in his eyes quickly fades as if I had given him a diagnosis that his dreams will never see the light of day.

"I have just never seen snow and can't wait to feel it."

Here he is, entering young adulthood in a foreign land, filled with new experiences, strange people and places to learn, and I have just taken away the excitement that he may not see the one thing he is looking forward to.

"We may still get some snow this year, you just never know. Being as it's January, we have had snow as late as March and even one year I remember a light dusting on the first day of April." I figure I should give him some hope that it could happen.

"Okay, well that is better. Maybe at least it will still come."

"I hope so."

"Yes, it is the one thing I really cannot wait to see here."

"If not, there is always snow in the mountains this time of year and they are only about an hour away. Maybe you can get someone to take you to the mountains to check it out."

"I will try, but I do not know who could do that."

"I hope we get some for you. It looks we like we are here, which house is yours?"

"It is the brick one."

Ken grabs his backpack which he had stowed between his feet and works his way up the driveway to his new home.

Two weeks later we will see the biggest snowstorm we have had in seven decades.

As the snow grounds me from driving and messes up all sorts of plans, I think about how many people may be excited to see and touch it for the first time.

This gives me some peace of mind, knowing that it is bringing joy to at least one person out there.

Accomplice

Her build matches her voice, soft small and easy to miss in a crowd. The white cardigan and long flowing cotton skirt she wears give her the look of the librarian in the original *Ghostbusters* movie.

Each step she takes announces to the world with a thunder, which her frail voice cannot, that her life is a painful struggle.

It messes with my mind to see the contradiction in appearance and age. She dresses and walks as though she is seventy-seven, though she cannot possibly be a day over twenty-eight.

"I'd like to go to Home Depot." Her vocal cords strain to push out.

"Sure thing."

Settling into the front seat seems to be the most stressful thing she has done today. Using both hands, she pulls the belt across her front to create the slowest click I have ever heard a seatbelt make.

"I need to pick something up and have you bring me back."

"No worries. I can wait while you go in."

Nothing more escapes her lips. Her stare is intense and straight forward the entire ride.

Before long we are at Home Depot and she is making the slow walk into the store while carefully deciding where to place every step on her way in.

As I wait, I check in on social media and rethink my decision to stay and wait. I feel guilty telling people to order a new ride. And honestly, if they are quick enough, I would be sitting in a parking lot waiting for my next call anyway.

She is actually faster than I expected. That, or I got lost in the time vacuum of social media and have no idea how long has really passed.

"How can her frail body push that thing?" I find myself asking as she is pushing a Rug Doctor carpet cleaner ahead of her.

"Let me put that in the trunk."

"Thanks. Now I just need to go back to the same place you picked me up."

"The motel?"

"Yes please."

Trying to not show surprise or judgment, I start the trek back to the motel, wondering what she might be cleaning up.

My mind races while her cold blank stare challenges the road ahead. Who gets a carpet cleaning machine for their motel room? How strong might she really be? Did she kill someone in there and now I am an accessory to murder after the fact?
I convince myself not to ask anything. No small talk. The less I know the better. This is not the first ride I have given where I decide this is a necessary course of action.

"Okay, here we are."

"Can you bring this up for me?"

We are parked right below the stairs that lead to the outside entrance to her room.

"Sure." She needs to kill the witness. I will make sure not to look in when she opens the door, and I will not let her get between me and the car. "Lead the way."

"It's right up here."

Setting the rug doctor down at the top of the stairs, I let it roll towards the door she is opening and quickly take a step back towards the safe retreat of the stairwell.

"Thanks for getting a ride. Have a good day."

"Thanks. I will need to take it back soon."

"Okay well, I may be close by."

"Great."

Getting back to the car, the first thing I do is go offline. This was enough crazy for one day.

Drinks

Pick up Michael at Tacoma Comedy Club. That is easy, I just walked out of there myself before settling into my car to drive a bit more.

Tacoma Comedy Club hosts an open mic every Wednesday which is a lot of fun. It is a free show and has a mix of professional and first-time comedians trying out their material.

"Ride for Michael?"

"Yes, that was really fast."

"Yeah, I actually just left the open mic and turned my app on."

"Oh, were you on stage?"

"No, not tonight. I do go up a lot, but it was not my turn tonight."

"That's cool. So you are a comedian?"

"Yes, I am. There is not a destination set, where would you like to go?"

"Anywhere good to get a drink."

"Have you been to Hanks?"

"Not yet. I just moved to Tacoma this year."

"Nice, well it is actually not far away and is a really cool bar tucked in the middle of a neighborhood in the old part of North Tacoma."

"That sounds perfect. Let's go there."

"It's so cool that you are a comedian. We go to the club a lot. We have probably seen you." This is the first time Michael's friend speaks up. "I'm Tamarahyah."

"So what got you into doing comedy?" Michael's curiosity is met with an enthusiasm that is charming.

"Well, I had a good friend who used to tell me I should try stand up because she thought I was funny. I would always say I am not 'stage-funny,' I am 'breakroom-funny,' and there's a difference! But eventually, I went through a bunch of changes in life and figured it was time to give it a try."

"How long have you been doing it?" Tamarahyah questions.

"I've been doing it over two years now."

"So are you a rideshare driver to pay the bills while you try to make it in stand up?" The pair seemed to pass the torch of being the interviewer with each question as Michael takes this one on.

"No actually. I love doing comedy, but it is really more of a fun hobby for me. I make just enough that it has turned into a hobby that pays for itself."

"So you drive full time?" breaking the pattern Michael asks a follow-up.

"No, I am building my own business as a speaker, coach, and author. I drive to help pay the bills while I get that kicked off the ground."

"Wow, sounds like you have a lot going on. This place looks really cool." Tamarahyah seems to like my recommendation as we pull up to Hank's.

"You should come in and have drinks with us!" Michael seems to not be ready to end the conversation.

"Really?"

"Yeah, totally. I love meeting new people and getting to hear their stories."

"I suppose I could do one drink."

"Sweet! Do you do this often with passengers?"

"No actually. I get lots of offers, but this is the first time I have taken someone up on it."

Michael and Tamarahyah have a naturally easy way of talking as we settle into a table across from the bar.

"What can I get you?" Michael asks from the bar as Tamarahyah and I secure a table a few feet away.

"I'll have a vodka cranberry."

"The same as always." She lets out as if just to make sure it's clear.

The conversation is natural and easy as if catching up with old friends who need to fill you in on what they have been up to the last ten years.

They ask more about my story. I share that at forty years old I came out of the closet and got divorced. Then after losing my job, I realized it was now or never if I was going to make my dream of being an author and motivational speaker come to life.

Tamarahyah shares that she is a travel nurse here for a few months working in the emergency room at the hospital. I was wrong in thinking they were a couple. In fact, she is best friends with Michael's girlfriend who lives a couple of hours away. While she is stationed here,

Tamarahyah is renting a unit in the fourplex Michael bought last year when he moved to Tacoma.

Michael opens up about how he was near the brink of ruin when he pulled together just enough money to relocate and buy this property. Moving to Tacoma was a fresh start and he has been getting to know the city and making lots of new friends along the way.

Three strangers in a bar getting into deep subjects, personal connections, and sharing a few laughs between the serious moments.

Before we know it, they are calling for last call.

"I can't believe we have been here for over three hours. Do you want one last round?" Michael plays the best host of the night.

"No thanks. I still have to drive. I'll take a water though."

"This is a great spot." Tamarahyah seems pleased with the new find.

"Yeah, we are going to have to come back here again."

Walking out to the car, Michael opens up his phone. "If I order a ride, will it go to you?"

"Seriously? I can just drop you off. You aren't going to buy me a drink and hang out for three hours and then pay me to take you home."

"That's cool. I didn't wanna make any assumptions."

Just a few minutes later we are in front of their place.

"Thanks for getting a ride and for an awesome night!"

"Thank you! It was so cool to get to know you."

"Yeah. I look forward to seeing you soon at the comedy club." Tamarahyah adds in.

"I will be there next Wednesday doing a set if you are free."

"We will be there!"

"Sweet! See you then!"

A week later I see Michael and Tamarahyah in the club for the open mic. This time I will be going up and hopefully they enjoy the show!

Gerald the Biker

Pick up Gerald flashes across my screen. I play a game sometimes. When there is a classic, formal name the person usually fits one of two characteristics. So I have started playing a game with myself on the way to pick them up where I guess: Old or Asian?

Gerald leans to the older side, but not as old as I might have guessed from his name. Maybe his mid to late fifties. He carries himself young and strong as he marches from the restaurant to the car.

"Andy?"

"Yes, Gerald right?"

"Yes, sir. How's your night?"

"Great thanks, just driving around town. How about yours?"

"It has been awesome. I used to live right across from this place and I would come in and drink, but now I am out in Tillicum. Where do you live?"

"I live in Tacoma."

"Tacoma? Nice." Gerald has a way of holding his gaze on me as he finishes each sentence. I feel the sense that he has a keen interest in me.

The night is darkening now. I can see the full moon glimpse from behind the clouds off and on throughout the drive as if peaking to see what is going on down below. Silence takes over the back seat. Then a quick sudden heavy breath giving away the idea that Gerald had fallen asleep and is now awake and alert again.

Thumping his open palm on the ceiling he seems lost.

"Do you need the light on?" This happens at times, as the control for the light is up front and out of the reach of backseat passengers.

"Yes." He answers as the car is illuminated from the small overhead light. "You are great." He is staring me down even harder now.

Gerald's hand reaches forward as if to give me a fist bump. I return the motion sending my fist into the back seat for a quick nudge. Just as our fists are about to collide, his palm opens up as if to accept a handshake. My hand naturally mirrors his and we shake. Actually, to be more specific, he shook my hand.

His hand was dry, but not a cracked skin and calloused kind of dry. A dry hand that is both warm, and strong. It is comforting, holding mine captive just long enough to say, I am alpha.

I am not sure why he needs the light on. He does not seem to be looking at anything from his wallet or looking for anything on the back seat. He only seems to be looking at me in fact.

So there we ride through the dark moonlit night, with my eyes on the road, and Gerald's eyes on me.

Something about the way he talks to me, the way he looks at me is intriguing. Something inside me woke up when he touched me. Something I didn't know was sleeping. We drive along, almost to his destination, an old bar close to his home called Galloping Gertie's.

"Are you meeting friends at the bar?"

"Oh yeah. Bunch of badass biker friends. That's my place."

"Sounds like a fun night."

Suddenly I feel his presence drawing in closer. The back of my right arm feels pressure, a gentle squeeze as if my bicep is getting a hug from his open fist.

"You are a great guy." Gerald smiles as he pulls his hand off my arm and slowly sinks back into his seat.

"Well thank you. You seem cool yourself."

"I try to be a good guy. But you are great."

"Thank you, sir. It looks like we are here."

"That seemed like a fast trip."

"I try to be efficient."

"You're great"

"Well thanks, you are all set."

Gerald seems to be deciding if leaving the car is what he really wants to do. Sitting perfectly upright with his phone in hand he looks straight forward at me.

"How do I tip you? You really deserve a tip."

"I can show you."

As I show Gerald where to go in his app to leave a tip, I get the feeling that he never looks down at the phone, only at me. "Got it."

"Okay. Thanks! Well, have a good night."

"Thanks. I hope you do too." He mutters as he works his strong body from the back of the car.

The last thing I see is Gerald wandering into the night as I drive away, with the moon once again taking a peak to see what it missed.

Drugs

Pick up at Walgreens.

It is odd to me that there is no name listed on this account, just a pick up location.

I could be more skeptical due to just how late it is, but Walgreens is open twenty-four hours so it could be someone out shopping, or an employee getting off of their shift.

Immediately my phone starts to ring.

"Hi, this is Andy."

"Hello, this is your next passenger request calling you."

"Yes, you are at the pharmacy correct."

"Well actually this is a third party service and we have a delivery for you to make if you are willing to accept the ride."

"Okay."

"We need you to go to the pharmacy, pick up a prescription, then deliver it to the address we give you. Are you willing to make this delivery?"

This seems interesting to me. My mind races with scenarios of just what I could be agreeing to, but I am more intrigued by where this ride could take me so I agree.

"Yes. No problem."

"Alright. I will text you the name and birthdate for the prescription after we hang up, as well as the address for the delivery. When you are there, you will need to go to building thirteen to make the delivery."

"Okay, I can do that."

"Perfect. When you are done, please text me the name of the nurse you hand the prescription to."

"Will do."

I am parking at the pharmacy by the time the conversation is over. In just another minute, my phone receives a text with a stranger's name and birthdate, as well as the address to make the drop.

This isn't the first time I have had to make a delivery. The last one was actually a rebuilt part for a diesel truck. I received a similar phone call that time with a request to go to a shop, head into will call, retrieve the part and then head to the address they would update in the app. Of course, that was not at one in the morning, and it was not someone's medication.

It will be a few minutes for the prescription to be ready. I buy a cookie while I wait. One of the health risks to this job is giving in to the temptation for junk food as it is often one of the only snacks available out on the road. And I have an overactive sweet tooth.

Taking the last bite of my chocolate chip cookie, I see the order is ready.

I had not paid much attention to the address sent over when I got the text, but as I type it into my GPS, it looks eerily familiar: 9601 Steilacoom Blvd SW.

It is not so much that I have the address memorized, as much as I know exactly where that is, Western State Hospital.

Now if you are not a local, you might not know that this is a mental hospital. Not only is it a mental hospital, but it also is a high security holding facility for inmates that are found not competent to stand trial. There has been more than one occasion when inmates have managed to get out. Just a few months ago two men escaped: one an accused murderer, and a second accused of assault.

I am sure it will be just fine I tell myself. It's now one thirty in the morning and this ride is spooking me just a bit.

It's not just the idea that Western State is a mental hospital, the grounds themselves give off an Alfred Hitchcock, horror movie vibe. Originally built in the late eighteen hundreds, the expansive grounds are scattered with remnants of the original army fort and buildings that were used here through the turn of the last century.

Pulling through the stone fence that lines the grounds and up to a row of would-be quaint brick buildings, some of which are over a hundred years old, I try to figure out where to go.

This facility is huge, like visiting a college campus, only in this case, half of the buildings are surrounded by fences with barbed wire running along the top.

The GPS brings me right to the front of the main building where an iron rod gate keeps me from going any further. Looking ahead I can see that the drive beyond the black bars leads into a central courtyard, surrounded by the old brick hospital. There is no call button, no guard station, no obvious place to go.

Putting the car in reverse, I figure I should try to drive around the main building and look for any signs of life. The white paper bag which is my passenger just needs to get home, so that I can be on my way.

As I skirt the perimeter of the main building, my headlights hit on signs along the main campus road, *Building 7* reads one sign.

"Of course! Now I remember." While my imagination had taken off into the *Twilight Zone,* I had forgotten that they said I need to go to building thirteen.

At least now I know where to go. If I can just follow the signs towards building thirteen.

It is so dark now. Driving further into the facility the road winds between towering evergreens and boarded up houses and buildings. These seem to be scattered between functional, yet lifeless buildings.

Finally, I see the sign I am looking for: *Building 13.*

The small windowless brick building is tucked back across a field with no immediate parking in front of it. I will have to park across the road and walk about thirty yards to the steel door which is the only entrance I can see.

There is no signage on the building itself. Next to the door is one small black button, about the size of a pencil eraser, in the center of a stainless steel panel with just a few holes above it.
My thumb depresses the button.

"Can I help you?" Comes through the small holes above the button.

"Yes, I have a prescription delivery for building thirteen."

"Thank you. I will be right there."

Something outside moves in the dark while I stand under the only light waiting for the voice to bring life to the door. Please let it be just the wind.

"Is this it?" The voice is familiar as the night guard opens up the steel door and stretches out her arm to take the prescription.

"Yes thank you."

"Thanks. Have a good night."

I have just enough time to read her name tag as the heavy door falls back into place between us.

Relieved that this task is over, but not out of the woods yet, literally, I speed-walk back to the refuge of my car. It's that walk you do when you want to look tough enough to not run away, yet inside you are scared to death of what could be moving in the shadows.

In the car, doors locked and pulling out between the stone gates that line the haunted grounds of Western State Hospital, I can now put distance between myself and the ride I just survived.

The Doggy Bitch

En Rama is another restaurant I haven't tried yet. I gave their chef a ride recently and he invited me in but I still need to do that. The way he described the crafting of their menu items made me want to leave my car in the street and go in for a meal right then.

Pulling up to En Rama I pull over as best I can to get out of traffic and wait for my passengers.

It is about three minutes before I see them make their way around the building from the side. Not sure if why they were over there or if the location was just loaded wrong, but here they are now so we can get on the road.

She looks frustrated. I wonder if it is because I was not parked right where they were waiting or if it's something else.

It is just like any other elevator ride at first. If you don't remember, those are the rides where they just get in and shut up.

"Ride for Adam, right?"

"Yes." She replies curtly.

"Soundview Drive?"

"Yes."

Silence.

Silence that is, other than the random mix of songs running through my *Driving Ditties* playlist. Like usual, the tunes of one ride can bounce from genre to genre and take the listeners on a roller coaster ride of musical variation.

As the music shifts from a country song, to *Nirvana*, then *Billy Joel,* and on to *Funky Divas,* I giggle to myself. My mind fixates on the irony of a silent couple being barraged with any random tune from the last sixty years.

A phone rings.

"Hello, Johnny."

I only hear her half of the conversation. This is a new pastime of mine as I drive around.

"We're on our way back right now."

"She's been alone for three and a half hours but we're almost home. She might have peed. Are you home now?"

"Is she okay?"

"Well I told Adam we had to leave but he didn't want to leave earlier. So we just left now."

"We're going to be home in a little bit."

"I know, I told him that we needed to go and that she couldn't be alone, but he didn't want to leave."

"Okay. We will see you in a little bit bye."

At least I know the frustration she was giving off was not because of where I parked.

"Well the dog's been freaking out and she peed and pooped on the floor because she's been alone for three and a half hours."

"What time did you say we needed to be home by?" This is the first time I hear his voice the entire ride.

"I said we need to be back at nine. She goes to bed at nine!"

"We are talking about fifteen minutes. We're going to be home at 9:15. And Johnny's already there."

"I said we needed to leave and you wouldn't go."

"I was waiting for the bill, it took forever to get the check."

"You could have given your dad the money and we could have just left. I would have just left."

"I am was not going to do that. We are talking about fifteen minutes here."

"Ya, well you just do not even care that she was home all alone and freaking out."

"Are you kidding me? It is five minutes after nine right now and Johnny is already there!"

"What difference does that make?"

"Even if we were home at nine, she would have been freaking out."

"I said we needed to go and you just would not listen to me. This is all your fault."

"Whatever! Just blame me. I don't care." He's done with this conversation.

Apparently so is she because now we have eight more minutes of silence as I exit the freeway to follow the road down to the Gig Harbor waterfront.

It is a gorgeous home. You know a home is nice when they have lights in the yard aimed at the trees just for effect.

I hear the click of a seatbelt unlatching as we pull into the driveway. They cannot get out of the car fast enough. If there was an option to use an ejector seat I imagine Adam would have used it.

"Thanks." Makes its way from her lips as she quickly hops out of the rear passenger door.

Adam makes a slower exit as if distancing himself from the threat of more conversation.

"Thanks for getting a ride." I leave off my usual, have a great night. It just doesn't quite feel appropriate.

Backing out of the drive I see their silhouettes keeping distance as they enter their gorgeous house overlooking the water and with the special lighting on their trees.

I cannot help but think not all castles feel like fairy tales on the inside.

Number One

"Ride for Hilary?"

"Yes, I am Andy. Thanks for getting a ride."

The Triple Knock is smack in the center of the busy part of Sixth Avenue's nightlife, making it a little congested at times when I try to pull up for passengers to load. Thankfully these two are ready to go and jump in quickly.

As Hilary slides across the back seat, her mother follows her in and takes the right rear seat.

"Does he know where to go?"

"Yes, Mom. It is loaded in the app already."

"Oh, that is cool. I am starving."

"Driver, do you mind if we go through a drive-thru?" Hilary asks.

"Sure, do you have a preference? It looks like the options on the way are Taco Bell or Jack In The Box."

"Let's do Jack."

"Alright. Got it."

It is not far at all to get to the drive-thru which only has a couple of cars in line. We just beat the rush as the bars are about to close down and all the drunks will want some greasy food to fight their soon to be hangovers.

"I have to pee."

"Seriously Mom?"

"Oh no. We are blocked in now." I feel like a parent taking my kids on a road trip. "Can you hold it?"

"They should have a bathroom here. Maybe I can just run in."

"Mom, only the drive-thru is open this late. They aren't going to let you in."

"It's worth a try. I gotta go bad!"

"Can we get two tacos, a large fry, a cheeseburger and an order of curly fries…"

"And can I come in and use your bathroom." Mom interrupts.

"Sorry, the lobby is closed. Was there anything else?"

"No that is it."

"Are you sure I can't use the bathroom?"

"Mom!"

"I gotta go."

The car is rocking from Hilary's Mom doing her 'hold it' dance while sitting in the back seat.

The smell of fried food fills the car as Hilary pulls the grease-stained bag through the window.

"Got everything?"

"Yes, all set."

Around the corner now, we start down Sixth Avenue as soon as the light turns green. Seeing blue lights in the rearview mirror, I pull over to let them pass.

To my surprise, the police car pulls up behind me and stops.

"I am so sorry ladies. It looks like he is pulling me over."

My windows have a dark tint so, I turn on the interior light and roll down all of the windows.

"Good evening officer."

"Hello. Can you tell me where you were going in such a hurry?"

"I am sorry officer, I'm a rideshare driver taking these ladies home. I didn't realize I had sped up so quickly."

Hilary's mom looks to the officer with a pleading look of fear. Had it not been that it was fear of peeing her pants, it would likely look suspicious.

"Yes, you were going forty-one in a thirty."

"Oh, I am sorry officer."

"Be sure to slow down."

And without taking my license or registration, he tells me to drive safe and have a good night.
"Thank you so much. You too."

"I did not think you were going that fast." Hilary's mom reassures me as we pull forward.

"Well, that makes me feel better. I have never actually been pulled over with passengers in the car before."

"We are almost there at least. You gonna make it Mom?"

"Yeah, I think I can."

Now I am left balancing the urge to speed and get there as fast as possible with the desire to stay out of trouble with the law.

Two turns later, one more red light, and we are pulling in front of their home.

"Thanks so much for getting a ride."

"Thank you!"

Exiting the car, they make their way inside. I laugh to myself as I watch Hilary's mom doing a jig in the light of the front porch while Hilary fumbles for her keys.

They left nothing in the car except the lingering smell of fast food and thankfully a dry back seat.

Give It Up for Gluten Free

He's guiding her to the car. I hope she's not so far gone that she might puke. That's always my fear with rides like this.

She can walk okay, yet she seems to be tripping on rocks that are not on the road, only in her mind.

Although I am not sure if he is sober enough to be much of a trusted guide, I still feel it's a good thing his hand is on her waist as they settle into the car.

"Heading back to the North End?"

"Yes, Oakes street right?"

"Yep!"

"That wasn't as bad as I thought it would be." I hear him direct towards her, obviously referring to the house party they just left.

"No. I didn't want to be rude, but I just couldn't trust eating any of the food."

"Yeah, the stuff I tried was good."

"Well it didn't look bad, but you know I can't risk what could be in anything. I had some veggies off the tray and that's it all night, so I'm starving."

"Maybe we should make a stop on the way home."

"I'd love to hit DOA and get one of their seared cauliflowers if the kitchen is still open."

"Okay. Let's see what time it is when we get closer." His voice turned my way. "Is it okay if we change the drop off to DOA?"

DOA, or Dirty Oscars Annex, is another local hot spot that has been featured on *Diners, Drive-ins and Dives*. It's on the east end of the stretch of bars and restaurants that run along Tacoma's popular Sixth Avenue district. It's not too far from their home and will be an easy detour to make at this point in the trip.

"Yeah, no problem. Just let me know when we get closer if you want to go there or home."

The conversation dulls as the music takes over the ride. Slowly their silhouettes combine into one in my rear view mirror, as she leans into his body, letting her head fall naturally on his chest.

The car is silent other than the background music that has become our playlist for the ride.

A rustle of jackets tells me there is movement behind me. Then I hear the distinct sound of lips opening and attempting to connect with another.

There is a very subtle variance in the tone and style of each of our lips as they open to kiss another. And it's possible to listen enough to hear if the kiss is being returned. His kiss is a heavier wetter sound while her return kiss is softer and dryer.

146

This pattern starts, wet kiss followed by soft dry return, followed by more wetter, and harder kisses. Soon more jackets rustle and the soft kisses seem to get lost in the movement.

Then suddenly the jacket shuffles abruptly as the one silhouette cracks down the center and once again become two.

"I'm not doing anything else."

"C'mon" is barely audible over more jacket rustling.

"I'm not in the mood"

One more jacket rustle and the start of a hard kiss before the crack in silhouettes opens up to form a wide valley, as each clings to opposite side windows.

"Just take us to the address in the system." Frustration weighs heavy in his voice.

"Really? So I don't get to eat now?"

"There's food at home."

"Come on, I just don't feel good." The negotiation comes through in her pouty tone. She speaks like a child begging for forgiveness after letting their parent down.

"I don't think we should go out if you're not feeling good." His justification seems to fool only himself, if even that. "Driver, just go to the home address."

"Whatever." Her resignation to the night's situation seems to speak past a one-night settlement.

I give a nod that I got the directions and nothing more.
Four silent moments later, we are in front of their home.

"Thanks for getting a ride."

As I watch him guide her up the walk to the front door, I am left to question where the line between caring and watching out for someone turns into control, dominance, and abuse.

Prep & Douche

Point Ruston is a beautiful new development on the waterfront where Tacoma meets up with the small town of Ruston. As I pull up to Wild Fin, the craziest couples of the night are heading my way.

Getting the two couples settled takes a minute as they figure who the largest person is. Generally, they win shotgun.

"She was not as bad as Roger's wife." Rear Right Female let's out.

"Oh totally, it was not painful like before. Awkward, but not nearly as bad." Replies Rear Left Female.

"Here we go" starts Middle Rear Male.

"You knew this was coming." Adds Shotgun Male.

And on the conversation goes for the first few minutes as they recount meeting the new boss's wife during the dinner they had just left.

This was pretty run of the mill for me in these types of rides: hearing the unfiltered opinions of folks when they let their guard down after the event. It's like being on the other end of a phone line when the wires would get crossed and you can hear your neighbors gossiping. Of course, no one under the age of forty will likely get the reference to crossed lines.

But at one point, Rear Right Female grabs Shotgun Male by the arm and says excitedly, "Did we clean up before we left?"

"Um, I don't remember, we were in such a hurry." He says with a slow and pondering tone. Then looks to me and says "Our aunt is babysitting."

"Oh, if you have kids I am sure a little mess, or a few dishes, are not a big deal."

Rear Right Female erupts in laughter. The type of laughter that tells me without a doubt that I have stumbled upon more than just a few dishes.

"I just hope she doesn't go into our bathroom."

Apparently, they were having a little adult fun before they left the house and may have left an enhancement device out.

"She would go looking just to try to find something to embarrass us with."

"Oh no." I do not know what to say and am trying to not let the laughter get in the way of my safe driving. "You should just try to think of the most shocking thing you could leave out for her to find then."

"That would be hard with her, she has left things out for us to find before on purpose when we went over to check on her dogs." Now that Right Rear Female is loosened up, she is on a roll. "Like one time, right on the counter was a glass butt plug."

"True!" Chimes in Shotgun Male. "Right there practically next to the note on what to feed the dogs."

By now the car is filled with laughter from everyone. Apparently, these coworkers are very close and perhaps work in a place where HR is very loose, or non-existent.

"I do not get that? It just seems nasty." Comes from Left Rear Female.

"Yeah, wouldn't it just be covered in…" Middle Rear Male pauses on his words, as if he is picturing what it would look like, and does not even want to say it. "…covered in shit?"

"Oh no. Not if you do it right." Right Rear Female is in full education mode now, as she has the attention of the entire car. "It's like my gay friend always says: 'Every time I even think I am gonna have sex I prepare. Prep and douche! Prep and douche baby!'" The accent and volume to which she adds to the last sentence bring a new level of rowdy to the conversation.

"I am sorry." Shotgun Male let's out in a low voice as he leans my way. "We've had just a few tonight."

"No worries man, it's more fun for me when people are out having a good time."

"Prep and douche! That's what he always says. Prep and douche. Prep and douche." Right Rear Female just cannot stop saying it. If you can imagine the flamboyant tone she is using, you will have a better understanding of the character she is playing at this point.

"Really? Wow?" Middle Rear Male is catching up from the shock of the idea of a plug that would go in what he considers an 'exit only' corridor.

"Guess that makes sense." Rear Left Female comes along.

"Prep and douche!" every time she says it, the car erupts in laughter. "You can say you learned something on one of your rides tonight."

"Oh yeah, very informative!"

As we pull into the front of their home, the rear seat empties into the driveway.

Before he exits, Shotgun Male leans over to me, "I am so sorry. I really hope she wasn't too much."

This is my turn to set him at ease. "Really nothing shocks me, besides, I'm gay anyway!"

"Really?!" as he erupts into a burst of surprised laughter. Rejoining the others I can see him pointing my way as he shares what I just told him.

As I back out of the drive, I hear the whole group break into laughter.

Then over the laughter, I drive away to the sound of Right Rear Female yelling at the top of her lungs:

"Prep and douche! Prep and douche baby! Prep and douche!"

Party

I am going to take a nap before I go to a party tonight. What are you doing? It is typical that I text with Cheri a bit between rides.

Just waiting for my next call. Kinda slow right now.

Bummer. Gotta make those bucks.

Yes, I do. Just got a call to the Murano. Have a nice nap!

The Murano is the place to stay in downtown Tacoma. A few years ago it was a failing Sheraton that towered above the newly built Greater Tacoma Convention Center. If you walked inside then, the eighties remnants would be a far cry from the bold artistic style you would be stepping into today.

"How are you guys tonight?"

"Great thanks! We are here celebrating."

"Nice! What's the big occasion?"

As the three middle-aged folks pile into the car, the lady half of the couple in back starts to explain.

"We came over from across the pass to celebrate his birthday."

"That sounds fun. And you're going to the Hitchin' Post?"

Now, don't get me wrong, I have no judgment on where people go to celebrate. It's just that the Hitchin' Post is a neighborhood dive bar on the border of NorthEast Tacoma and Federal Way. This is about fifteen minutes from downtown and seems a random choice for out of towners.

"Oh, we used to live near there and it was our regular hang out."

"Oh cool. My friend goes there all the time. I have even met her there a couple of times to hang out."

"Who is your friend?"

"Her name is Cheri."

"Cheri Hardman?"

"Yes, actually that is her."

"So funny, she is coming to the party tonight."

"Really? I was just texting with her and she mentioned going to something. What a small world!"

"She is very funny. Did you know she does stand-up comedy?"

"Yes, actually that is how we met."

"Seriously, do you do stand-up too?"

"I do. Cheri is one of my favorites. Not just as a comedian but a good friend too. We have done some shows and carpooled together a lot."
"Have you seen her show on YouTube?"

"Yes, *Heavy Petting*, I just got to be on it last week. Well, we filmed it last week. I think my episode comes out in another week or two."

Heavy Petting is a show that Cheri has created on YouTube where she interviews local comedians about their dating stories while also showing off their pets. Since I do not have a pet of my own, I got to go with her to the animal rescue to help their pets find forever homes by being featured on her show.

As we cross through the tide flats making our way through the port, and up the hill to the residential part of Northeast Tacoma, I learn more about their weekend trip, how long ago they moved away, and how much fun they had in the good old days at the Hitchin' Post.

She does almost all of the talking. Just the occasional agreement from her husband the birthday boy, or a joke from his brother riding shotgun.

"We surprised him flying his brother out from across the country for this weekend."

"That is really awesome."

"They have not seen each other in ten years."

"So I bet you were really surprised."

"Yes completely." This is the first time I have heard Husband speak more than two words.

"I got home from work and he was sitting in my recliner."

"He did not even see me there for like five minutes." Now, Brother starts to add his part to the story.

"It wasn't that long."

"I just can't imagine someone being in your house and you not seeing them right when you walk in."

"He was too busy giving me a kiss."

"It just felt like old times right away, like you fit right in and should be there I guess."

"I suppose that makes sense." I figure I should add something into the conversation by this point.

"You should come in and party with us." Once Husband opened up, he kept going.

"Really? That might be fun."

"Cheri would sure be surprised." Lady Half is back in the chat now.

"Yes, she would be. I do have to drive more tonight, but I could come in for a bit."

"Awesome! We get to party with the rideshare driver on my birthday."

Pulling into the gravel lot I find a convenient spot close to the door. If there was not a close spot, I would drop my passengers off at the door and then catch up with them inside.

"Are you stalking me?" It's the typical kind of thing Cheri would say if I just showed up in her regular haunting grounds.

"This was our driver." Lady Half jumps in.

"Whoa, what a small world."

"Yeah, and they said I could party with y'all."

It is not the hardest I have partied for sure, not drinking with a crowd that is ready to party it up makes for a less fun time on my part. But I have to keep driving to get to my number for the night. Catching up with Cheri for a bit and getting to know her friends even more before I get back on the road is fun.

As the karaoke fires up in the background, I take my leave. I see the timing is right. If I am going to stay longer, I will need to have a drink or two and that will rule out driving the rest of the night.

Though the temptation is there, I say my goodbyes and get back on the road.

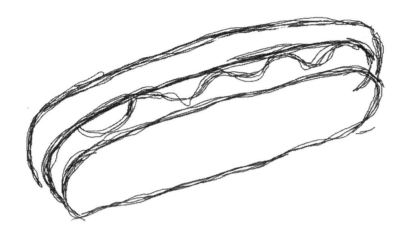

Weiner

Pick up Laura comes across the app. I have been to this motel several times. This strip on Hosmer is a popular spot for people to stay when they are in town for concerts at the dome. It's just close enough to downtown to be convenient, but far enough away to be a bit more affordable.

Just confirming I have arrived at your motel.

Whenever I do not see someone waiting outside I text right away so that I do not waste time trying to find them.

Four minutes later a long flowing skirt and cardigan make their way down the exposed stairway towards the car.

The cold stare and soft shaky voice recall in me the eerie feelings I had the last time I was here six weeks ago.

Some riders you never see again. Some randomly pop up over and over again. And some just show up out of the blue just when you have put them to the back of your mind.

"Heading over to the church?"

"Yes. I just need to be dropped off there."

"Sounds great."

The relief in my voice has to come through, though I try to hide it as I find myself back in the car with the same cold stare, and glad that it will just be a drop off this time.

Entering the car, her smell takes over the vehicle. It is not her that gives off the smell, but what she carries. In her hand is a small clear sandwich bag with what appears to be a microwaved hot dog.

"Please let it be a hot dog and not a body part!" I think to myself.

It is a short trip to the church. The car holds the stillness and the lifeless silence of a frozen January pond the entire way.

Nothing happens with the extremity in the bag. Her stare, like before remains fixated on the road ahead.

"Here we are. Do you know which entrance you want to use?"

"Around to the back is perfect."

"Great, back where we are out of view from the road." I think to myself. "Well, I have lived this long!"

Pulling around to the far side of the church, I see a welcome sight: other cars and people heading in.

"Here you go. Thanks for getting a ride."

"Thank you."

Step by careful step, she makes her way into the back entrance of the church hall with her microwaved wiener in her hand.

And that is the last I will ever see of Laura, the motel murderer.

Dana & Dad

Black Star is a local bar on the main drag of Pacific Avenue on the south side of town. It always seems to be a lively spot.

Pick up Dana runs across my screen as I wait for her to make her way out. It can take a few minutes some times. At a busy bar, I never know if they are waiting to close out, or if they even hear the notice that their driver has arrived.

Soon a young and rough looking man makes his way towards my car followed by, what I can only imagine, is what he might look like forty years in the future. The pair pause next to the car as if stumped on what to do next.

Without warning, the female version of the rough young man appears and marches directly from the bar to the back passenger door of my car.

"What are you waiting for? Get in!"

And on command, with no reply, the men get in the car too. Old-n-Rough sits up front while Dana sits in the back with Young-n-Rough.

"Driver, can we make a stop at the quickie mart?" Dana asks.

"Sure thing. Just let me know which one." They are heading home to Parkland which is a straight shot down the busy Pacific Avenue. I imagine in the three-mile stretch there are about twenty options for gas stations and convenience stores sprinkled between the bars, fast food, pawn shops, and a strip club.

"What do you need?" Rough-n-Young lets out.

"Beer."

"Good. I'm not done drinking."

"Well, you're not drinking all of my beer again. You can get your own."

"I never drink all your beer."

"Yeah. You do!"

This does not sound like the first time they have had this conversation. It sounds like a conversation that started as kids about who ate all the candy and now has evolved into an argument over beer and cigarettes.

"You can get your own. This one is great right here. We still have twenty minutes."

It's now 1:40 am and by Washington state law, all alcohol sales are cut off between the hours of two and six am. Pulling over to the store, the two adult kids get out for their beer as Old-n-Rough stays behind.

"You need anything Dad?" Dana barks through the closed door.

His head shakes to the negative.

"Do you ever go to the casino?" Old-n-Rough casts my way.

"Not too often, but every once in a while I will meet friends there."

"Think I'm going tonight."

Just a few minutes later and Dana is back with Young-n-Rough, each lugging along an eighteen pack of Bud Light for their own personal consumption.

"All set?" I confirm as they settle in.

"I want to go to the casino."

"Dad, I'm not going to the casino tonight. We just got beer."

"You don't have to go. But I'm going."

"How you think you're going to get there?"

"Rideshare."

"Dad, you can't go. How you gonna get home? I won't be there to order a ride back for you." She sounded genuinely worried about his well-being. There is a plea in her voice that comes through as part worried daughter, and part overly dramatic drunk.

"I'll catch a cab."

"Are you sure you're going to be okay? Do you promise to call me when you're ready to come home so I know you are on your way?"

"Christ girl. I'm not a child. But yes, if you'll feel better I'll call you."

"Driver, can you drop him off after you take us home?"

"Sure thing."

It really makes no difference to me as I will have to wait for the next ride request to come through anyway, plus run the risk of getting someone even drunker for a passenger.

As Dana gets out of the car with her Bud Light and Young-n-Rough follows suit with his, Old-n-Rough turns to me. "Alright, you know where the casino is?"

163

"Most of them, which one do you want to go to?" There are several casinos in the area, some larger than others. Being as we are now in Spanaway, the closest are the smaller casinos in Lakewood.

"The Macau"

"Oh yeah, I know right where that is." The Macau is on the smaller scale of the local options but it seems to be very popular. The pagoda style roof and ornate gate you pull through to enter the parking lot makes it a landmark hard to miss along the edge of the Korean International District on South Tacoma Way.

"I'll just throw some money down on the tables and see how long I can last."

"Seems like a fun way to pass the time."

Before I know it we are pulling through the entrance into the lot.

"Thanks for getting a ride. I hope the tables are good to you."

As Old-n-Rough closes the car door behind him, my phone lights up for the next ride. Seventeen minutes away back in downtown, but the fare is at almost triple the regular rate, so I decide to take it.

"Thanks for getting a ride!" My standard greeting lets out again.

"Thanks for getting us." He says.

"Oops, somebody left a phone back here." She opens up.

Turning my head, I recognize the glittery gold case. "Oh no! That was my last passengers. Thanks. I'll get it back to her."

Dana will be beside herself without a way for her dad to call her.

"We are headed back to Gig Harbor." He confirms.

"I hear that rideshare drivers don't like to come to the Harbor." She shares.

Gig Harbor is a quaint little town across the Narrows Bridge from Tacoma. Its roots as a small fishing village grew into a trendy place to live over the last few decades. Getting over the bridge and into town is a good ten to fifteen-minute drive from the city.

"Oh really? That's the first I've heard of that."

"Yes, it took us a while to get a driver to come to get us. And you know, we are usually going into the city so it's a good trip."

"I guess I could see it being hard sometimes. Speaking for myself, I don't have a problem going to Gig Harbor at all, but I usually try to take trips that are within ten minutes away so that would rule out crossing the bridge to do the initial pick up."

"I guess that kinda makes sense."

"But once I'm there, I drive there all I can and I'm happy to go wherever the passenger needs to go."

Taking these two from downtown Tacoma and home to Gig Harbor, means it will be about an hour before I can get back through the city again to Spanaway to return Dana's phone.

We have a pleasant chat as they tell me about catching up with old friends and watching the live bands tonight at The Swiss, where I picked them up.

Soon enough I drop them off on a dark wooded street which is what most of the forested setting of Gig Harbor is like.

"Now back to Dana." I think to myself. "What are my options?"

There is an option in the app to report a lost item. But what good is that going to do? The notification will go to her phone and that is in my hands! I can go to the Casino and search out Old-n-Rough, I am sure he is still there. But what if he loses it? Besides, Dana will not be able to get a hold of him if he has her phone, and she will be beside herself with drunken-daughter worry.

165

No, the choice is clear. I have to go back to the house and knock on the door. Well, if there are lights on I will, that is. From the conversation between Dana and Young-n-Rough, they were going to be busy with their own packs of Bud Light well into the night.

It gets deeper and deeper into the night before I am finally back on their street. I recognize the welcome sign at the end of the block which looks like it was very welcoming when the paint was fresh. Now it seems to be more of a reminder that this is home, whether you like it or not.

It's a small street where each of the row houses are the same nondescript color of light grey. The only distinction as to which house is which is to notice the car parked in front of each doorway. Theirs has a blue Ford pickup from the eighties. You remember the kind with the chrome tailgate and the black stripe across the back? I remember when I dropped them off that this looked like the truck that was probably Old-n-Rough's pride and joy in his prime, and now it may be that he lets Young-n-Rough use it under extreme need, but probably not. Old men rarely trust anyone with their trucks.

The lights are on. Even though it is a cold winter night, or morning actually, as it is now after 3:00 am, their windows are open. This makes it seem less threatening for me to knock. Stepping onto the one-stair wooden porch, I am greeted with the chatter of reruns blaring on the television.

I knock.

"Someone's here." Dana is surprised, as anyone would be at this hour. "Who the hell is it?" I do not imagine the hour, or alcohol have had much influence on her speech.

"I have your phone. I was your rideshare driver." I project through the open window.

The door opens quickly with a relieved looking Dana, on the verge of tears. "Oh my god! Thank you so much! I was so worried I was looking everywhere for it."

"I was worried about just coming by so late, but I knew you would be waiting to hear from your dad and without your phone, I had no way to let you know."

"You are the best. I wish I had something to give you for bringing it back."

"It's no worry. I am just glad I was able to get it back to you."

"Thank you! Thank you!" Her arms surrounded me in a huge hug of gratitude. "I'd give you ten out of five stars if they'd let me!"

"You're welcome."

And my work for the night is done. Time for me to go home, get to bed, and start over tomorrow.

Jim

Pick up Jim at UP Station displays on my phone.

UP Station is a neighborhood bar in University Place. A small town which straddles Tacoma on one side and the Puget Sound on the other, University Place was named for a university that once owned property there, but never developed. It was put on the world map in 2015 for hosting the US Open at Chambers Bay Golf Course.

Chambers is beautiful. It's a links-style course that was developed on the land of a former gravel quarry right along the water, with views of the Olympic Mountains, the Puget Sound, the Narrows Bridge, and beautiful sunsets. It's not only popular with golfers. There is also a path that circles the perimeter for joggers and walkers.

Anyway, back to the bar. Arriving at UP Station, I press the notification to let Jim know I have arrived. *Be right out.* Comes through as a text. At least I know he is aware.

Seven minutes, and three texts later, Jim and his crew make their way out of the bar and into the car. Jim, a slim but built mid-thirties version of Matthew McConaughey, sits up front while his buddies, Drunk and Drunker take up the back seat.

"Headed to Rein Haus." Jim confirms with a sly inviting smile. It was the type of smile which could pull you in or scare you away, depending on the person sending it your way. It was a smile I could not pull off myself without coming across as a lonely middle-aged creeper.

"Sounds great! Having a fun night?"

"Yes, well mostly. Not so much for this guy." Jim points back to Drunker directly behind him.

"Not at all for him." Drunk adds on.

"Oh, sorry to hear that."

"Woman problems!" Jim explains. "We finally get this guy out for a few drinks and you would think that he left her and moved across the country with another woman."

A cell phone rings in the back. The volume gets louder as Drunker pulls it from his jeans pocket.

"Hello." His voice is suddenly serious and somber. "No, I only had one at UP Station and now we are going…"

Both Jim and Drunk start shaking their heads and holding their hands up as if saying, do not tell her where we are going!

"…we are going downtown."

It's a stretch. Rein Haus is a German-themed restaurant and bar that is one of the newer additions to Tacoma's historic Stadium district. It is near downtown but about a mile away.

A sigh of relief is felt in Jim and Drunk, while the stress level of Drunker just seems to be getting higher and higher. The pressure of keeping her at bay, of trying to act like the soberest person in the car, the tension of his friends not wanting to have her ruin their night, all seem to be getting to him.

His conversation seems to go on for several more minutes but his contribution is limited to the occasional *uh huh, yeah, nah,* or *you know I love you baby.*

"Oh my FUCKING god!" apparently he is off the phone now. "She is the one who told me to go out and now she has called me six times. SIX FUCKING TIMES! Asking when I am going to be home? It's only eight FUCKING thirty!"

"Woman issues!" Jim reminds me as if it needs to be said again.

"Well, at least you know she wants you." It was all I could think to say.

"More like wants to be like…" Drunker has a way of tripping over his words halfway through his sentences as if he keeps forgetting where he was going. "…like wants to keep me prisoner."

Drunk chimes in at this point. "It was supposed to be Jim's big night out but Drunker really needs it more."

"You would think she would leave me alone just long enough to celebrate my friend's…" it seems like the longer the sentence the harder it is for him to complete.

"Jim's birthday." Drunk finishes for him.

"Awesome, happy birthday!"

"Thanks"

"And it looks like we are here. I appreciate you guys getting a ride."

"You should come in and have a drink with us!" Jim's invite is accompanied by that sly half smile again.

"I would really love to, but I have to keep driving."

"Really, look there's a spot right there. It was meant to be."

I do not know what to say. I would love to hang with Jim and his smile. But I am pretty sure he is only drunk-inviting me. That coupled with the idea that this is my first ride of the night and I cannot afford to just give up the rest of the night's income.

"I really would love to but I can't take the time off right now." It hurts to say the truth to Jim and watch his smile fade to acceptance.

I honestly do not think he is interested in anything more than a drink with his driver and a story to share later, or I would give up the money to hang with him.

But my radar for these things always fails me, so I am left to wonder if there was more behind his request and the sly half smiles he threw my way along the ride.

Disturbing

It starts like so many rides. Driving down the street to a craftsman home at the end of the lane, along the border where suburbs turn into fields of long since forgotten apple orchards, I see the cluster of cars that shout out, *the event is here.*

I have arrived at your address.

It's a simple text to let them know that I have arrived. I have had many passengers say the app is slow to alert them that their driver has arrived, so I like to get the timer going right away.

The dark night hides any of the home and yard's blemishes well. What is not covered by darkness sparkles with the glow of the small white lights strung through the trees and along the fence-line. Makeshift folding tables are disguised with white linen table cloths, and wine glasses seem to be scattered throughout every surface.

This had to be a wedding. There is something about weddings that seems to elevate the appearance of everything and even everyone.

The otherwise cluttered yard, the untrimmed hedges, the saw-horse tables, all gleaming in white linen and lights give off a glow of elegance. Tuxedos and gowns seem to flit through the scene as the last few guests gather their essentials to be on their way.

Who will it be, I wonder? And that is when I see him tripping over the small rock border that edges the garden between my car and the event.

"Hello, sir. Andy right?"

"Yes."

"She is looking for her shoes and then we can get on our way. I am sorry for the wait sir."

It has been seven minutes now. Long enough that the timer alerted me to cancel and collect my no-show fee two minutes ago.

"No worries. Fun party?" I try not to make the assumption that it was a wedding. I have been wrong before and have learned that there are many different reasons why people may go all out for an event that I had never thought of.

"Her sister got married."

"Oh cool! Looks like it was a beautiful wedding."

"Yes, it was great. I am going to go see where she is." And just like that, prince charming wanders back up the lawn and into the glow of twinkly white lights in his so perfectly fitted tuxedo, loosened by a night of partying and made even hotter by the undone tie hanging from his collar.

It was like watching clips from a movie. I would see him fade out of sight, then suddenly reappear. Then cross the yard towards a gown propping up a drunken bridesmaid. Mumbled words are exchanged before he crosses the yard again, back to the void of darkness by the main house. Then in a fairytale move that only a proper prince charming would do, he brings Cinderella her shoes.

Shoes in his right hand and Cinderella clinging to his left shoulder, Charming navigates the lawn.

"Careful, there are rocks here that are hard to see."

I may have mistaken his earlier stumble to be more alcohol influenced than it actually was.

"Right here, watch your step."

There is a way in which a man talks to his woman that will tell you everything about the type of man he is. He speaks not in a condescending, impatient way, but with such care and concern. Not a whiny baby talk way either, but a confident, dominant, in charge of your care, concern. I cannot imagine anyone that would not want to be cared for the way Charming cares for his drunken Cinderella.

As I start the ride and navigate my way through the twisted roads to get out of the Sumner neighborhood I confirm that we are headed back to Steilacoom, about thirty minutes southwest.

"I can mix up the music if you want anything different."

"We are good with anything sir. Thank you." His voice is deep, polite, and oddly familiar. Maybe it is the politeness and the use of sir, that reminds me of the many military men I have given rides to over the last couple of years. Maybe there is something else.

Cinderella reminds us of her state constantly. "I apologize. I do not usually drink this much, but it was my sister's wedding."

"It looks like it was an amazing wedding."

"It was. But I do not know if my toast was any good."

"Baby, you were amazing."

"No, I totally fucked it up. I was supposed to say the thing about how much she was my other half and now she has..." The unreasonable tears of alcohol well up in her eyes keeping Cinderella's words from finishing. "I am sorry, I drank more than usual. It was my sister's wedding."

"It's okay baby. You are doing just fine." His words are once again caring, confident and in charge.

"No, it's not. He probably hates us. We are probably the worst ride ever and then he's going to rate you with one star, all because of me."

"Trust me, you guys are totally awesome. I have had some riders I did not enjoy and you guys are not on that list."

"See baby. You are okay."

"I just can't believe it. I am totally the drunk bridesmaid."

Now, I could not argue with that.

There are a few different ways to get to any place typically and tonight's route has us driving west on highway 512 until it ends at South Tacoma Way, where we will exit to city roads for the rest of the trip into Steilacoom.

The stop light at the end of the highway makes its change from red to green, but before I can move my foot from one pedal to another, a sea of blue lights races our direction from the left. There is an urgency in the speed of the cops that tells me this is a more than just backup being called to a scene.

Something big must be going down.

It is enough to trigger Cinderella.

"I hope we are not in trouble for being drunk." She is not even being sarcastic. She is actually worried.

"We are okay baby, that is why we used a rideshare." There is a reassurance and again a familiarity in his voice that is so very soothing.

Then I finally make the connection. Twenty minutes of "It's okay baby" and "I have you taken care of" and I finally place him.

His voice is a carbon copy of a friend I made a year ago. We hung out for a bit, and while I had hoped for more, friends was all it was meant to be. But the voice, the caring confidence, it is all there.

So this is how we finally make our turn to head through Lakewood towards Steilacoom: Charming holding it together, while Cinderella and I are both triggered by his voice.

It's only about a mile down the road until we need to make our next turn. But before we get to the intersection, we are passed by another two police cars racing past with lights and sirens on full blast.

"Oh no. Something big must be going on." It is a natural response. I forgot about Cinderella's state.

"This is so awful, we should not be drunk right now. Something serious is going on."

"It's okay, the police will take care of whatever it is, and Andy here is going to get us safely home."

"But I just feel like it's such a waste. That I just partied all night and real things are happening in the world."

She has a point that I think we all feel at times. What right do we have at happiness or entertainment when there are injustices, pain, and hunger in the world? Yet to live a somber life, just due to the fact that everyone is not in the same place, only serves to bring the world down and not up.

We will all have times where we can celebrate and times where life is hard, even tragic. So to not celebrate the good moments only gives more power to the bad.

We are close to the scene now. I had hoped that the blue lights would have fled further up South Tacoma Way towards the city and away from our course, but this was not the case.

177

Looking ahead, I only see blue lights, and they seem to surround the entire intersection we need to get through in order to get to our destination.

Slowing down. I assess the situation and figure out where we can go from here. There is nowhere to turn between the intersection and us.

I suddenly find myself pulling right up to the scene. In the middle of the scene is more like it.

Blue lights form a border around the entire intersection. Officers just leaping from their cars as they arrive. An SUV which seems to have been stopped only by a very sturdy and tall light post pours steam and smoke out of the crashed engine. The lack of any red lights or traffic control tells me this has just happened.

Then looking down, I see them.

Bodies.

First I see the body of a person next to the SUV, as an officer kneels next to them, checking for signs of life. This is a sobering sight: an officer kneeling to hold the life of another human being as they take their last breath.

Next, my eyes catch sight of another officer running across the intersection as fast as she can to start CPR on a second body lying alone on the cold, hard, unforgiving pavement. It is a split second view that will forever be stamped in my memory.

"Oh my god, what just happened" Cinderella is distraught now, as I do everything I can to keep calm and move to the right lane in order to skirt the edge of the intersection, which is our only option to get out of this scene.

"This is awful."

Her words are spoken with such hysteria I am now worried she may have an actual panic attack before we get her home. My own disturbance by the scene will have to be put on hold momentarily.

"Baby, the police are there doing everything they can." His reassurance is interrupted by a glare of red lights as aid cars fly towards us before disappearing into my rear view mirror. "Everything is going to be okay"

"Did you see that? There were people dying!" Heavy breathing interrupts her words as she forces them out through tears of hysteria fueled by her drunken emotional state. "This is not right. I am just drunk and we are out partying while people are dying. We can't even help."

It is true there can sometimes be no worse feeling than that of helplessness when others are in need, and you want to be there for them. It's the pain of seeing a friend in tragedy when you have no means to lift them up and all you can offer are words or to lend an ear.

She is in a really bad state now, and the detour around the scene of the accident just added another five minutes to our ride.

The road ahead is blurring as tears well in my eyes. I just want to pull over and stop driving, but that is not an option, at least not until these two are home.

"I can't believe this." Cinderella is almost hyperventilating.

"Do you have a favorite song or artist I could play that might ease things?"

"Good idea." Charming says with his confident, reassuring voice. "Baby what do you want to hear?"

"I just can't even think about music when people might be dying right now and I am just drunk in a car."

"Can you play *Tim McGraw* by Taylor Swift?"

Takes me a minute to get it typed in the search bar, but soon enough the song is playing and it seems to help. It is a good distraction, music.

Music transcends the rational part of our brain and speaks directly to our emotions through our subconscious mind. This is why, when you watch the sad dog-rescue commercials, before you even see the first visual cue, your brain is feeling emotional. It works to both bring you down, and lift you up. Next time you're feeling down, slow, or lacking motivation, put on your favorite upbeat song and see how quickly your mood lifts.

As *Tim McGraw* plays along Cinderella's nerves seem to settle. No longer do I hear the heavy breathing or constant sighs as she tries to grasp control of her drunk reality. Only the sound of Taylor Swift and the occasional soothing tone of Charming's caring voice guide us down the road through the very dark night.

"This is almost over, should I let it shuffle Taylor Swift."

"That will be perfect, thank you, sir."

Taylor gets us back to their house without any further excitement from Cinderella.

"Can you please pull up next to the truck on the left?"

"Sure thing. I hope you guys get settled in and get some rest tonight."

"You too, that is definitely going to be on our minds."

"Thank you for being a really cool driver. Please don't give him a bad rating because I am drunk."

"Baby, he said he likes us."

"I know, but I am drunk and there was all that stuff and I just don't want to mess things up."

"It's all good, you are fine. See, I am pushing the five-star rating right now."

"You'r the best. Drive safe, sir."

"Thanks, I think it is straight home for me now."

"Understandable. Have a good night."

"Thanks. You too."

"Goodnight Mr. Rideshare! Sorry I was drunk."

Up the driveway they walk to put an end to their night, so they can start over safely tomorrow morning.

Pulling away, my phone alerts me with my next ride, but I decline the ride and go offline. My ride home will be somber and reflective, wondering if this may have been another driver's last night on the road.

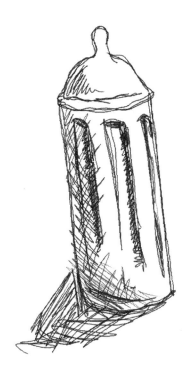

Nips

Pick up Jessica at Steel Creek scrolls across my screen telling me it is time to mobilize once again.

Ending the YouTube video I am watching, I start up my playlist of songs for while I drive and pull out of the empty parking lot that was home for the last twenty minutes.

"Jessica right?"

"Yes, Andy?"

"Yep. Thanks for getting a ride.

Once again, nothing very exciting or original here. It's just how so many of these encounters begin.

If they would be dressed more formally, and about fifteen years younger, I would say they are drunken bridesmaids. But their demeanor speaks for them, it's more like a drunken bridesmaids' reunion.

"It's our ladies night out!" pours from Jessica's mouth almost as loosely as the bartender must have poured her drinks.

It's not a surprise, the girls I pick up here always seem to have been out for a good time. It's a country bar thing I have found to be true.

Jessica grabs the front seat while the three other maids fill up the back.

Pulling away from Steel Creek, which is a whiskey bar in downtown, I remember that I still need to get down here for one of their Thursday night line dancing events with a few of my friends. My dancing is not the best, but with some good whiskey, I am sure I will improve.

"How is your night going?" Flows from the back seat.

"Great thanks! Just out driving around all night."

"We are having such a blast." I cannot tell who is talking. They all sound the same. But this voice sounded further to the right than the last.

"Those guys were totally hitting on us."

"Yeah well…" there is a pause as I hear a shuffling in the back. "…still got it!"

"What was that guy's name? He gave me his number."

"Which one? The last one?"

"Tee shirt guy?"

"Yeah, I need to text him and thank him for a good night."

"Wasn't his name John?"

"No John was the guy with the really tight jeans."

"Are you sure."

"Yes remember because he said I am John like it was some big deal."

184

"Oh yeah, that's right!"

"I am here and I am John." The maid tries to make her voice as deep as possible, but her laughter disrupts her imitation.

"Tee shirt guy, what was his name?"

"What was on his tee shirt?" I just have to know why he earned this nickname.

"Oh, it wasn't what was *on* his tee shirt. It's what was *in* his shirt."

"Oh, gotcha."

"Muscles!"

"And nipples. Don't tell me you couldn't see those things poking out."

"I didn't mind. I was looking at the pecs." She leans forward from the center back seat as if to say just to me: "His shirt was so tight, I could see every muscle moving underneath."

"And Nipple!" Her friend adds from behind me.

"Yes, every nipple." Jessica echoes. "Did you tell him that your nipples are pierced?"

"We didn't get there, but I know he won't mind."

"Yeah right, some of those country boys can spook like a horse by a snake."

"Well, he won't mind when he sees what they do."

"What the…"

"You know how arousing it has been since I got these things pierced?"

"Whatever. You always say that kind of stuff."

"Seriously, just from touching them now I get worked up. Whoa…see"

185

"What is going on back there?" Jessica turns to see what is happening in the back seat.

From the corner of my eye, I can see that the maid on the far right is reaching over and has her hand on the chest of the maid in the middle.

"Aaaah… see, I lose control when you touch it."

"You guys are such lesbians." Jessica chimes in.

"What if we do both?" Now the left rear maid seems to want to get in on the action.

"Aaaah! Whoa!" It seems like a moan of excitement mixed with pleasure and shock all coming out at once.

"You guys are going to get us kicked out of our rideshare. Or worse yet, get me a bad rating!"

"Are you kidding me, Jessica? I bet he likes it. I bet he's gonna go home happy as fuck tonight."

"Whoa!" The gals seemed to have not stopped taking their friend for a ride. "Oh yeah, baby!"

"I'm sorry my friends are crazy. And apparently horny."

"You're good. I see some pretty crazy shit."

"I bet nothing like this."

"True, I think this is the first time I have had gals getting it on in the back seat."

"Oh my god! You two are going to make me orgasm just from that."

"You are faking it."

"You know she's faking it!"

"I am not. Whoa! Do that again."

"Come on, we all know how much practice you got at faking it that whole year you dated Jared."

"I had to do something! He didn't know how to work anything, and he just would not give up. Oh yes, that's it girls!"

"Seriously, is this the craziest ride you have had?"

"It's up there."

"He likes it and you know it."

"It is definitely entertaining."

"See, I knew it. Sick fucker." This is ironic coming from the woman getting her nipples twisted in the back seat.

"Entertaining yes, but not arousing."

"Yeah right creep."

"Sorry, you are just not so much my type."

"Because I'm too hot or what?"

"You are a good looking lady, just not my style."

"So who is your type? Which one of us would you pick?"

"Looks like this must be the place. Is that the right house on the left?"

"Yes, this is it right here." Jessica seems ready to go but her friend in the back is on a mission now. I may have slightly offended her by saying she is not my type.

"Well, I am not getting out 'til you at least tell me what your type actually is. Who would you pick?"

"C'mon. Let's go."

"No! I wanna know."

"It's no big deal to me."

"Fine then, who are you into. Which one would you pick?"

"None of y'all sorry to say." I feel like maybe they all leaned in a bit after I let this out. Not an *I'm interested tell me more* way, but more like a *ready to pounce* way.

"Really?"

"Well, I would have to say that I would go for someone more like tee shirt guy."

"Huh?" Nipple gal is confused.

"Yeah, you know, a hot cowboy in a tight tee shirt and jeans, where you can see every muscle moving underneath."

"Gay! You're gay?" Jessica lets out through rolls of laughter as she looks back to nipple girl. "Boy do you know how to hit on all the wrong guys."

"I do not! Besides, I wasn't hitting on him."

"Maybe you were not hitting on the rideshare guy, but you have a history."

"Oh no!" I let out through a laugh as they start to pile out of the car. "Well, you guys have a great night!"

As the four bridesmaids finish their reunion and laugh their way into the house, I pull forward, rolling down my windows to let the smell of whiskey and cheap perfume air out.

Don't Go

Michael walks towards my car, well one of them is Michael at least.

"Michael right?"

Whether it is the baseball caps, plain t-shirts or the Carhartt jackets, I cannot be sure, but their entire look can be summed up in one word: bro.

"Yes, well he is anyway." The early thirties dude, Bro One, points to his friend. "Still waiting on the girls."

Michael takes the front seat while Bro One takes the rear passenger seat and waits for the girls to catch up.

Soon enough the female version of the bros, the chicks, make their way toward the car. These are not party chicks. They are not clutching a small wallet-sized purse and doing the quick high-heel shuffle speed walk down the drive. No, these are bar chicks, jersey shirts, jeans, and Converse. Dressed to hang with the guys, shoot pool, throw darts and have some shots.

Whenever it's bros and bar chicks, it can be so hard to tell who is dating, who might be brother and sister, or who is actually just hooking up.

"We are heading to the Hard Luck." Michael confirms.

"Sounds great."

It is going to be a stretch to get there before last call. It should only be a five-minute ride, but it is already 1:30 and some bars will make their last call as early as 1:35.

"We just want to get a couple of shots in before the night is up."

"Great! You guys having a fun night?" At this point, I should apologize to the readers. My lack of creativity in the opening conversations on each ride does have a tendency to get repetitive.

"Drinking!" adds in Chick One from the seat directly behind me.

"So hell yeah!" chimes in Chick Two from the center back seat. "Take a left right here."

"Where are you taking him?" Michael knows we are in a hurry.

"Trust me this way is so much faster to get out of here."

Their home was easy enough to get to with no surprises, but even neighborhoods you drive through every day can have hidden twists and turns with secret cul-de-sacs tucked away in their own private oasis known only to the micro-locals, the people who live on or right next to such streets. Tonight I was finding one of these, right in the otherwise straightforward neighborhood of South Tacoma.

"Now go right at the end of the white fence."

"Right here?"

"Oh, no one more block then right."

"Are you sure you know where you are going?" Michael seems the soberest, and most aware of the time constraint to get to the bar.

"Yes, Trish showed me this way and I use it all the time. Okay here, go right. Then left at the stop sign in a couple of blocks."

"Got it." By the time we reach the stop sign, I recognize it as Yakima Avenue which will put us on course for a straight shot to the bar.

"See this way we skip that light that can take five minutes to get through for a left turn."

"Okay, but why didn't you say that at the beginning?" Michael was on board now but annoyed at the process.

"Just need to get there for a couple more shots." Bro One opened up now that we were on course. "Do you get any crazy passengers?"

"Oh yeah, I definitely have my share."

"What's the wildest ride you have had so far?"

This question is the most commonly asked question, right up there with, *is this your only job.* So I have a few stories that I keep top of mind. I have just enough time to tell them about the Responsible Drunk, and the Motel Clean-up Lady before we are making the turn into the lot at the Hard Luck.

Bro One has been the most intrigued by the stories and, while there has been plenty of banter with everyone, he has taken the lead in the questions for the trip. "So how does it work, will we get you again for the ride back?"

"Well, it usually would send me a ride request by then for my next trip."

"Can you just hang here so we can get you again?"

"If it was just like three to five minutes it would not be a big deal, but it's a pretty busy time so I would be missing rides."

I have seen this before, where people think they can be in and out quickly and then ten minutes later, I am left wondering whether I should stay or go. And those are only in the cases where the person did not leave their crap in my car, forcing me to either leave it on the curb or go in to get them.

"Oh it will be longer than that, we may play a game of darts while we are here." Chick One chimes in as the voice of reason.

"What if you just came in and I bought you a couple of shots while you waited?"

"Well that would be nice of you, but then I wouldn't be able to drive anymore."

"Oh yeah. Well, what if I gave you five bucks to wait?" Bro One is on a mission.

"I can hang for a bit and see what happens, but if it sends me a request I should take it. You never know, sometimes it is a while between rides and sometimes they are right away."

"Well is there some way we can get you to stay? What if I gave you a blowjob?"

Shocked laughter slips out of my mouth as the rest of the car seems to share the same surprise.

"Well, that is a hell of an offer."

"He probably would too." Michael seems to either know his friend well or just enjoy the banter.

"Uh huh." Both Chick One and Chick Two reinforce in unison.

Did anyone else catch on to the fact that his negotiation jumped from five bucks to a blow job? Which now leaves me to wonder how good a blow job it could really be if it is only one step up from five dollars.

"Seriously, he probably would do it." Michael seems to really think this is a possibility.

"As nice as that offer is man, I should get on the road. You never know though, I could still be in the neighborhood when you are ready to go home."

"Alright, if you are sure."

"Yeah."

"Well okay then. Maybe we will see you soon."

"Maybe. Thanks for getting a ride, and have fun!"

"Yeah man. I hope we do see you in a bit."

"Never know."

"Thanks for the ride." Michael and the chicks echo as they walk up towards the bar just in time for last call.

It is prime time for people to be going home as bars all over town are announcing last call and guests are closing out their tabs and ordering rideshares.

By the time I see them taking their seats at a table near the door, my phone is lighting up with a request for my next passenger a few miles away at the U Betcha Pub.

Local

Hey Andy, It's Tim from BD Local. When you get a chance can you please call me? I have an opportunity I would like to discuss.

What a great way to start the morning on the first day of my birthday month! I have not even gotten out of bed yet and this is the first message on my phone.

Sure thing. Are you free in about an hour?

Sounds great. Talk to you then.

"Hey there."

"Hey, Tim. How are you?"

"Great thanks. How have you been?"

"Good thanks. Staying busy like always, but all good."

"Well the reason I was reaching out to you, is that I am going to be hosting a radio show starting next week and I am looking for a co-host."

"Oh wow! That sounds really cool. What is the show about?"

"You know how we have the BD Local app where we feature local businesses?"

"Yeah, of course."

"Well this show is going to be called *Be The Better Local,* and we are going to interview different business owners, community leaders, and entertainers every week. It is like the app comes to life over the radio, and live as a podcast on Facebook."

"That sounds really awesome."

"Well when we decided we needed a co-host, I thought of you because I knew of your experience with your podcast, and with everything you are doing in your business, I felt like it would be a great fit."

"I am really honored that you would think of me."

"Well is it something you think you would be interested in doing?"

"Yes for sure!"

"Let's get together this weekend for coffee and chat about details and see what we can work out."

"Awesome. I will text you the times when I am free."

"Great. I look forward to it."

"Me too."

One week later we will be on the air live producing the first ever *Be The Better Local* radio show and podcast.

You can check out this week's show live as well as all the past episodes by looking up the BD Local page on Facebook.

Last Chapter Party

Join me Saturday night as we live the last chapter of my book before I write it. The ultimate choose your own adventure party as we rideshare from bar to bar, one hour per stop through town from six until close!

This is the message I post for all of my friends.

I have been capturing stories and adventures as a driver, but have not had many experiences as a passenger. Tonight is going to be that night.

I have mapped out a route through town which will take us to some of my favorite hot spots. Stopping for only an hour per location before we load up the rideshares and head out to the next one.

"Ride for Andy?"

"Yes, thank you." Feels weird to have the role reversed as myself and a friend load into the car for what he refers to as Andy Vargo night.

"Heading over to The Ale House?"

"Yes, we are going to hit lots of spots tonight but this is stop one."

"He's writing a book!" My friend shares for me.

197

"Nice. What is it about?"

"I am also a rideshare driver, and it is going to be a collection of my stories."

"Nice."

"Tonight we are going to be passengers all night, and that will be the last chapter."

"Cool!"

She is personable and good to talk to. No crazy story to share, but off to a good start.

"Here is your first stop of the night!"

"Thanks so much for the ride."

"I hope you have a fun night, and good luck with the book!"

"Thanks, drive safe!"

Arriving at The Ale House, there is a table started already in the back. Some family is already here and a couple of friends are making their way in at the same time that I arrive.

"Hey everyone! Thanks so much for making it!"

It is low key at first, introducing friends to family, pouring the first drinks and answering questions about what the plan really is for tonight.

Another friend joins in and we have now expanded the tables to connect four tables together. It is fun to get out with people I do not always have the chance to hang with.

My nerves are not loosened up yet as I am still getting used to the idea that I have invited everyone from different elements of my life: family, school friends, work friends, and even gay friends.

Four quadrants I had until recently kept very separate. The idea that I need to just be me, the same authentic me, in front of all of them at once had brought my nerves to a high the last few days leading up to this event. But this is me now, and the more I accept myself and become okay with these situations, the better life seems to get.

"It's been an hour, time to order your rideshares! Next stop Seven Seas!"

My one job for the night is to keep us on schedule, and going to the right places I had posted in my invite, in case others want to join in along the way.

Our next driver is an elevator operator. He confirms where we are going, operates the machine and says little more beyond that. I cannot say that he is rude, just not conversational by any means. The eight-minute ride feels more like fifteen minutes.

Seven Seas is an awesome venue. Inside, the large open warehouse style room is filled with rustic wood furniture surrounding the bar. Off to the sides are a Valhalla Coffee location and food available from Built.

The second stop still feels a bit mellow. We are just warming up and everyone is getting to know each other more. We lose one person who only had time for stop one but we gain another, so the numbers stay even.

Someone buys me a beer.

We visit.

This place is full tonight. So we push a couple of high top tables together. A few people can sit, while the rest of us stand centered around the group.

"It's already been an hour. Ready for the next stop?"

This one seems to have flown by. Barely enough time to get through a drink and have much time to chat. Next time, we may have to order our rides a little sooner so that we do not cut into the arrival time.

"How is your night going?" Our driver for this leg of the trip seems to be happy to have some conversation.

"Great, we are just hopping from bar to bar through Tacoma."

"That sounds like a fun night."

"Do not worry, we are not that drunk yet."

"You seemed alright to me."

The Hub is a straight shot along Market Street then around the block to the back of the building, so before we know it we are there.

No crazy story, no freaky driver, just a quick, pleasant ride to our destination.

Between Seven Seas and The Hub, a couple of people peel off and head home, while we pick up three more friends along the way. The numbers are staying even, a mix of ten-twelve people throughout the night.

"We are going to get some food here." One couple shares as we arrive at The Hub.

"Good idea. This is a great spot for that."

Not only is The Hub a great spot to eat, but the timing is also perfect. Having been drinking for a couple of hours now, I need to get some food in my belly.

Then someone buys me a drink before the food arrives, then another once the food comes. I try to pace myself, but each friend wants their turn getting a drink for me. And I cannot be rude, can I?

We make the decision to skip a location in order to accommodate for a longer stay here while the food is prepared and eaten.

Opening up my phone I pull up the event and add a message: *Staying at the Hub longer and skipping the next stop. Going straight to The Parkway next.*

By the time we are loading up the rideshares to get to the next destination, I am having a hard time documenting the journey. But I am not having a hard time relaxing and having fun. The anxiety of pulling all four of my friend quadrants together seems to have been long forgotten.

Our car arrives first at The Parkway Tavern. This is going to have to be a quick stop. We are already behind schedule and have skipped a stop to make up for it. But I love this bar and wanted to make sure it was still a part of the night.

We luck out. There is a table that just opened up right by the bar. The group seems to have it down by now: order a round and close out right away.

The group seems to chat and mix well now that we have been a few places together, and have broken bread together. Food and drink will melt the toughest rivalries, and lighten the most awkward moments.

"Time to go! Order your rides to E-9!"

E-9 has been a Tacoma hot spot for as long as I can remember. It is actually the bar that my brothers, brothers-in-law, and Dad brought me to for beers when I turned twenty-one. It is Tacoma's original craft brewery and one of the oldest breweries in the state. E-9 is short for Engine House Nine, as it is housed in an old fire station.

"Who knew they were having karaoke tonight?" I say as we arrive.

The food from earlier helped, but I am feeling very comfortable by this time of the night.

"That might be fun." Friends seem to chime in all together.

Taking the center row of tables our group gets their drinks in hand as we settle in for another round in a new place.

"How are you guys doing tonight?" I am comfortable enough to make friends with the strangers at the table behind us now.

"We are great thanks. How are you?" I do not pick up on the snicker in her voice saying she is just humoring a drunk old man.

"Awesome thank you!" Just out hitting bars with all of these cool people. My hand opens up as if to for the first time reveal the table of friends I had hidden behind me.

A few of my friends wave while I am sure they are rolling their eyes out of my sight.

"Hey there." My new friend waves to my table.

"Love your hair! It is just the right color of blue."

"Thanks."

"And I am not being a smart ass. I have a way of saying things that sound like I am being an ass when I am totally serious. I love it."

Her friends are laughing a bit at the exchange. The other gal across the table catches my eye. "And I love yours too, Red. Have you guys noticed that everyone at this table has a different color of hair?"

Turning back to my table I try to bring my friends into the conversation, not wanting to be rude. "Hey, have you guys met my new friends, Blonde, Brown, Blue and Red?"

"Well, that's not really our names." Blue lets out with a smile. "I am Audrey and this is Jake."

"And I am Alice and this is Sean." Red tags on.

"Nice to meet you all. I'm Andy. You guys should do karaoke!"

Heading up to put my name on the list, I think through what song to even do. There is an art to picking a karaoke song that is fun, that you can sing, and that isn't way too long. I fail at this tonight.

"Hey, are you guys having a fun night?" Having put my name on the list to sing *American Pie,* I meet the table on the other side of ours.

"Yes, we are. It looks like you are too."

"I am."

This is a table for two with a good looking couple, maybe in their early thirties.

"Are you guys gonna do karaoke?"

"I am not." She says.

"I doubt it." Comes from the good looking gentleman sitting with what I really hope is his sister.

"Dang, well think about it and I will come back to you."

Back to the center table now, I am checking in with my party. I have to say that this is where the details get a little fuzzy.

Staying at E-9 for karaoke. Next stop will be Odd Otter at 1 am. I update my event. I am at least keeping on task with letting people know where and when they could find us.

"Andy, you're up. *American Pie.*"

Here goes nothing. If you have had just enough karaoke juice, your voice sounds great to you, no matter how the rest of the world may receive it. I sounded great. I rock that song. A friend even joins me for part of it.

"Nice job." Blue gives me a nod as I get back to my table.

"Thanks! You gonna get up there Blue?"

"Nah, I'm good."

"Alright. How about you Red? Blonde? Brown?" They laugh every time I use their hair color as their names. "I am just kidding, Audrey, Alice, Sean, and Jake."

"Wow, how did you remember those?"

"I try to pay attention, and I am not as far gone as it may seem. But it is more fun to say Blue, Red, Blonde, and Brown!"

"Well as long as you remember our real names I'll play along."

"Sweet! I am Andy. Did I mention that already?"

"Yes, actually." Blue giggles.

Before I sit back down with the group I check in with the couple who I assume are related. I feel better if I assume they are related at least.

"Okay, what's your name? I am going to put *Piano Man* on the list for us to sing."

"Trevor."

"Really! You gonna sing with me Trevor?"

"That song I might do. We will see."

"Okay. But I am going to put your name on the list so you are going to have to."

Now I settle back down with my group. We are all still here except the few that we lost after The Hub.

I am not adding anything into my consumption at this point. Just water while I banter with the tables around us and then check back in with my group.

Friends from my table get up and sing karaoke. Other friends who did not know each other before tonight are visiting.

"It's time to get Andy back up here, this time with Trevor. Andy and Trevor singing *Piano Man*."

Looking back across the bar, I see Trevor looking my way. He gets up and starts to head towards the mic.

"Awesome! Glad you aren't ditching me."

"Well, they said my name so I had to."

"Except that no one else really knows your name so you could have ignored it."

"Wish I would have thought of that!"

He is a good sport. We sing for the group and do not do half bad.

"Hate to say it but we gotta hit the road." The first friend to call it a night lets me know.

"Awe okay."

It becomes the permission the others need to make their way out too. It has been over six hours at this point and most of them have hung in there the whole way.

"Alright then, well I am going to order a ride down to Odd Otter in case anyone wants to make the last stop."

"I'm in." My one diehard friend moves to the front of the line.

"Ride for Andy?" One more ride back to downtown.

"Yeppers!"

"Where are you going?" His reply is short and bold.

"Do you know where Odd Otter is?"

"No."

"I can tell you how to get there. It's is downtown on Pacific."

"I need to type it into the GPS."

"If you must, but I can tell you too."

"I have to type it in for the ride to work."

"You know it just tracks where the car goes to charge the ride right?"

"I have to type it into my GPS."

"Okay well, it's Odd Otter, on Pacific, right across the street from the Matador."

I do not want to rock anyone's world. Besides, I am sure he just figures I am wasted and have no idea what I am talking about.

"I will type it into my GPS."

"No shit!" I think to myself. Looking back to my one remaining friend for the night. We exchange that look of this is gonna be interesting.

A silent five-minute ride later and we pull up to Odd Otter. I have ended many nights here, it is not too big, really laid back, and the staff is really friendly. There always seems to be a great mix of people coming and going as well.

Arriving just a bit before last call, we have time for one last drink before the lights go dark on my night of adventures.

"Thanks for staying with me to the end!"

"Of course! I wouldn't miss it."

"Now we just gotta get home." Pulling out my phone, I open up the app to order that one last rideshare of the night.

She is friendly, normal, talkative. "How are you guys doing tonight?"

"Great thanks." As we stumble into her clean car.

"Heading home?"

"Yes. Been out since six hopping from bar to bar."

"Wow! You started early."

"Yes, well we wanted to go to a bunch of different spots."

"That sounds like a fun night."

"Yep. I am gonna write a book about it."

"Great!"

I am a little disappointed that none of my drivers for the night are crazy. I have no wild rideshare driver stories to share of them freaking me out or offering me anything insane.

But then it hits me. What if we were their crazy story for the night? What if I acted a bit goofier than I remember?

Either way, it was a fun night!

"Looks like this is it right?" She says pulling up to the end of the driveway.

"Yes. This is perfect right here."

"Thanks for getting a ride!"

"Thank you for driving. And be sure to drive safe!"

And that brings us to the end.

Until the next ride…

Parked

It has been three years, five thousand rides, countless hours and miles. Sure, other drivers have driven more. Others have far crazier stories. But these are my drives and my stories, from my town.

It's time for me to park the car and get out to all these places for myself. This ride has given me a collection of stories, some crazy misadventures, and a fun night out with friends to continue writing our own story. I've made new connections who I still see around town, and some that I honestly try to avoid, like the motel-killer-wiener-lady!

Unexpectedly I learned a lot in my time as a rideshare driver. Not just about where to go in this great city, but I came to appreciate the community that I live in even more than I already did.

I learned that sometimes you need to lend an extra hand, even if it is outside of your assigned job. I learned that most people are interested in getting to know others around them. And most importantly I learned that there can be fun in every part of your day if you know where to look and keep an open mind.

I never met Mr. Right, or if I did, he walked out of my life without us knowing that we shared a ride. But I did meet many people who became…

…just another one of my many One Drive Stands.

Local Hot Spots

There are so many great places around town and unfortunately, not all of them made it into one of the stories in this book but all of these great local hot spots that I visited on my rides are worth stopping in to. So, to do justice to them I have included a list of the places I visited the most in this great city. There is no accident as to why they are on this list, they are also some of the most fun places to check out in Tacoma.

Restaurants & Cafes

Anthem Coffee & Tea
Antique Sandwich Co
Art House Café
Asado
Bluebeard Coffee
Boathouse 19
Cooks Tavern
Corina Bakery
El Borracho
En Rama
The Fish Peddler
Frisko Freeze
Gateway to India
Happy Belly
Honey at Alma Mater
Indo Asian Street Eatery
Indochine
Johnny's Dock
Knapp's
Lefty's Burger Shack
Mandolin Sushi & Steak House
Marcia's Silver Spoon Cafe
Memo's Mexican Food
Moctezuma's
MSM Deli
Old Milwaukee Café

Over the Moon Café
Pacific Grill
Pine Cone Café
Pomodoro Italian
Primo Grill
Rosewood Cafe
Shakabrah Java
Shake Shake Shake
Southern Kitchen
Southern Pacific
Stink Cheese & Meat
The Table
Valhalla Coffee Co
WildFin American Grill
Wild Orchid
Wooden City
Zodiac Supper Club

Clubs & Bars

1022
1111
2121
7 Seas
The Ale House
Airport Tavern
The Beach Tavern
Black Fleet Brewery
Black Star
Bob's Java Jive
Brewers Row
Camp Bar
Cassidy's
Cheers
Church Cantina
Cloverleaf
Cole's
Cook's Tavern
Crown Bar
Dawsons
Devil's Reef
Dirty Oscar's Annex
Dorky's Arcade
Doyle's
Dystopian State
Edison City Ale House
Engine House 9
Flying Boots & Wings
The Forum
Galloping Gertie's
Half Pint
Hanks
The Hard Luck
The Harmon
Hitchin' Post
The Hob Nob
The Hub
Jazzbones
Katie Downs
Knapps Lounge
La Ca Bar

Lattitude 84
The Loose Wheel
Magoos Annex
The Matador
Matriarch Lounge
McMenamins Elks Temple
Meconi's
The Mix
The Mule Tavern
New Frontier
Northend Social Club
O'Malley's
Odd Otter
The Office
Pacific Brewing
The Parkway Tavern
Peaks & Pints
Pint Defiance
The Plaid Pig
The Red Hot
Rein Haus
Rock The Dock
The Silverstone
The Social Bar
The Spar
Spud's Pizza Parlor
State Street Beer Co
Steel Creek
Steilacoom Tavern
The Swiss
Tacoma Comedy Club
Terry's Office Tavern
Tipsy Tomato
The Top of Tacoma
The Triple Knock
U Betcha
Unicorn Tavern
UP Station
Valley Tavern
The West End
Wingman Brewery

Entertainment & Interests

Alma Mater
The Blue Mouse Theater
Cheney Stadium
Freighthouse Square
The Glass Museum
The Grand Cinema
LeMay Car Museum
Murano Hotel
The Pantages
Point Defiance Park
Point Ruston
Real Art Tacoma
Reign FC
Washington State History Museum

Ruston Way
Stadium High School
Stadium Thriftway
Tacoma Art Museum
Tacoma Comedy Club
Tacoma Defiance Soccer
Tacoma Musical Playhouse
Tacoma Rainiers Baseball
Tower Lanes
Uncorked Canvas
Union Station
Wag Pet Market
Wright Park
The Rialto

Weed Shops

Cannabis Oasis
Clear Choice Cannabis
Commencement Bay Cannabis
Tacoma House of Cannabis
Diamond Green
Emerald Leaves

The Gallery
The Herbal Gardens
Mary Mart
Urban Bud
World of Weed
Zips Cannabis

Casinos

Emerald Queen Casino
Great American Casino

Chips Casino
Macau Casino

About the Author

A native of Tacoma, Andy Vargo does a lot more than just shuttle people around town!

If you ever feel awkward about yourself, then you can understand how Andy Vargo lived the first forty years of his life. Coming out of the closet at forty doesn't define him, pursuing his passion to help others does. When he is not driving folks around town, Andy works corporate and school events as a motivational speaker and helps people live their fullest lives as a one on one life coach. At night you can find him working stages around the northwest as a comedian making light of his journey with the gift of laughter. Awkward is not only his brand, but his style as Andy encourages us all to 'Own Our Awkward' and be true to our genuine selves.

Andy hosts the podcast, *Own Your Awkward*, co-hosts the *Be The Better Local Show* on *BD Local* and shares thoughts and ideas in his blog and video series available at awkwardcareer.com.

more books from **ANDY VARGO**

Choose your focus and improve your life with the Awkward Journal series from Andy Vargo.

Each guided journal follows the same principal that you can pick one thing to focus on and follow three simple steps each day to make your life be the life you want!

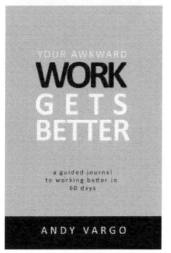

Made in the USA
Columbia, SC
08 June 2019